A Rabbi Looks at Jesus of Nazareth

A Rabbi Looks at Jesus of Nazareth

JONATHAN BERNIS

Chosen
a division of Baker Publishing Group
Grand Rapids, Michigan

Published by Chosen Books
11400 Hampshire Avenue South
Bloomington, Minnesota 55438

Chosen Books is a division of
Baker Publishing Group, Grand Rapids, Michigan.

Printed in the United States of America

In keeping with biblical principles of
creation stewardship, Baker Publishing Group advocates the responsible
use of our natural resources. As a
member of the Green Press Initiative,
our company uses recycled paper
when possible. The text paper of
this book is comprised of 30% post-
consumer waste.

Library of Congress Cataloging-in-Publication Data

Bernis, Jonathan.
    A rabbi looks at Jesus of Nazareth / Jonathan Bernis.
        p.   cm.
    Includes bibliographical references (p.   ).
    ISBN 978-0-8007-9517-7 (hardcover : alk. paper) — ISBN 978-0-8007-9506-1 (pbk. :
alk. paper)
    1. Jesus Christ—Messiahship. 2. Jesus Christ—Historicity. 3. Jesus Christ—Person
and offices. 4. Messianic Judaism. I. Title.
    BT230.B46   2010
    232—dc22

                                                                      2010036936

*To two men of God who reached out to me and planted
the seed of faith:*

*First to David Toth, who saw something in me worth investing his
time into. Your perseverance and patience as well as the example
of your own life made a great impact on me.*

*And second, to the Young Life counselor who challenged me to ask
God to reveal the truth to me about Jesus, all those years ago as
a teenager at Camp Silver Cliff in Colorado. I do not remember
your name, but you played a vital role in my coming to faith.
Thank you for being bold enough to confront me. You challenged
me to keep an open mind, to find the truth for myself.
I am forever grateful.*

Contents

Acknowledgments

My deep gratitude to the wonderful people who have worked so diligently to bring this project to completion—*thank you!*

To my beautiful wife, Elisangela, and my precious children. You always greet me with wide-eyed enthusiasm—an excitement that is punctuated with those most special of all words, "Papai's home!" *I love you more than life!*

To my staff at Jewish Voice Ministries International. The faithful execution of your duties during this writing discipline made it possible for me to devote the time necessary to complete this book. *You are the best!*

To Dave Wimbish, Mary Ellen Breitwiser, Grace Sarber and Jane Campbell for driving this project and me to the finish line. *I could not have done it without you!*

For the friends of Jewish Voice whose faithful financial and prayer support is a constant source of encouragement to me. *I am forever thankful.*

Most of all, to my beloved Yeshua HaMashiach. *Thank You for redeeming my life.*

Acknowledgements

Introduction

A QUESTION THAT DEMANDS AN ANSWER

WHO IS JESUS OF NAZARETH?

All of history hangs on the answer to that question. It is a question that has divided the world for the past two thousand years. Is Jesus the Messiah, the Son of God—as the world's two billion Christians believe? Or is He a lunatic and liar who deceived the masses?

If you are reading this book, chances are you have chosen to stand with the world's two billion believers in Jesus the Messiah. But some people try to remain neutral. They say they do not really know where they stand with regard to Jesus' claims of divinity, but they do believe He was a great teacher. Regarding this "neutral" approach, the great apologist C. S. Lewis said:

> I am trying here to prevent anyone saying the really foolish
> thing that people often say about Him: 'I am ready to accept

Jesus as a great moral teacher, but I do not accept His claim to be God' . . . A man who was merely a man and said the sort of things Jesus said would not be a great moral teacher. He would either be a lunatic—on the level with the man who says he is a poached egg—or else he would be the Devil of Hell. You must make your choice. Either this Man was, and is, the Son of God, or else a madman or something worse. . . . Now it seems to me obvious that He was neither a lunatic nor a fiend: and consequently, however strange or terrifying or unlikely it may seem, I have to accept the view that He was and is God.[1]

No matter how hard people may try to remain "neutral" about Jesus, you know as well as I that it just does not work. One cannot study the New Testament and come away thinking that Jesus was just "a great teacher and a good man." If He was simply a good teacher, why did He refer to Himself as "the bread of life (John 6:35)," "the light of the world" (John 8:12) or "the way and the truth and the life"? (John 14:6). He was either a lunatic and liar or He was and is who He claimed to be. After all is said and done, a person must either accept Him or reject Him for who He claimed to be. There is no middle ground.

Sooner or later everyone has to take sides in the "Who is Jesus of Nazareth?" debate. He demands it. He even confronted His own disciples, asking them point blank: "Who do you say I am?" (Mark 8:29).

If you are a believer in Jesus, you have already chosen your side. If not, I challenge you to read this book with an open mind and make your own decision.

In the pages ahead I will seek to answer this question, first by sharing a little of my own journey. Then we will look at the findings of scholars who have delved into the life of Jesus. We will consider the historical evidence. We also will study what Jesus' contemporaries had to say about Him. But before we go further, I need to make a few things clear:

1. I assume you are reading this book either because you are a believer, or you are a Jewish person who is interested in discovering the truth about Jesus.

As I said earlier, it is impossible not to have a bias about Jesus. When it comes to matters of faith, most of us believe what our parents taught us. We may deviate from our parents' teachings at some point in our lives, but most of us "come back around" to the worldview we learned as children.

That is not the case with me. The worldview I hold now is far different from the one I knew as a child. I have undergone a dramatic paradigm shift. If not, I would not be writing this book. When my experience did not match up with my previous beliefs, I was forced to discard those beliefs. Conversely, when experience validated the truth of things I had always been taught *not* to believe, I had no choice but to believe them. I must therefore honestly admit that I am writing with a definite point of view that is influenced by my own personal pilgrimage in search of truth.

Having admitted my bias, I will still claim that my aim in writing this book is to give an accurate, responsible and respectful presentation of the historical facts concerning Jesus of Nazareth. I also hope to present these facts in the simplest possible language. I am not interested in writing a scholarly treatise that can be understood only by those who have a doctorate in theology. Nevertheless, this book is based upon years of research and study. I will draw from the ancient Hebrew Scriptures as well as the New Testament. I will provide evidence from history and science. I will look at the Talmud—the collected teachings of ancient Jewish rabbis that form the centerpiece of modern rabbinic Judaism. I also will explain how rabbinic Judaism differs from biblical Judaism. And I will show what many great people, Jews and non-Jews alike, have had to say about Jesus of Nazareth after taking a close look at His life and teachings.

It is my fervent prayer that all of the things I present in this book will help you to find and share the truth about who Jesus of Nazareth was and is.

2. I want you to understand what I mean when I refer to myself as a rabbi.

I am a Messianic rabbi. In other words, if you ask a mainstream rabbi about me, he or she will probably tell you that I am not a "legitimate" rabbi. Why? *Rabbi* in the modern Jewish world indicates someone who has studied at a recognized Jewish institution and has been ordained by a mainstream, recognized Jewish body.

Although I do not meet these criteria, I am ordained and have served in ministry for more than 25 years. I am credentialed since 1984, by one of two recognized national Messianic Jewish organizations. I also have an extensive background in theology, as well as in the studies of Judaism and Christianity that would meet the educational criteria of many traditional rabbis. I also lived and studied in Israel during my last year of undergraduate study, working on several archeological excavations. Furthermore, I am fiercely proud of my Jewish heritage and use the title *rabbi* to assert that I am a practicing Jew, even though mainstream Jewish leaders would disagree.

Let me also remind those who would dispute my credentials that the word *rabbi* means "teacher." In fact, ultra-Orthodox rabbis are ordained as a result of training and mentoring, rather than earning post-graduate degrees from accredited Jewish institutions.

3. Some things cannot be proved or disproved.

If you are expecting me to help you prove beyond any reasonable doubt that Jesus is or is not the Messiah, then you will be disappointed. I cannot prove that, nor can I prove that the Bible is the inspired Word of God. I also cannot prove the existence of God.

What I *can* and *will* help you do is present a thorough examination of the evidence that might help someone to believe in Jesus as the Messiah. In other words, I will show you that it takes more faith *not* to believe in Jesus than it does to believe in Him.

But no matter how much evidence there may be—and I believe there is plenty—it still comes down to faith. Study and research can take one only so far. There is still a gap, a distance that can be covered only by taking a leap of faith. This is the gap between head knowledge and heart knowledge. It is the distance between hopelessness and hope, between mortality and eternal life.

Most of those who accept the claims of Jesus have done so not because they have researched the evidence, but because they have had a spiritual encounter. This was my experience. It was not my study of the Scriptures that turned my heart toward Jesus. Rather, it was my encounter with Jesus that sent me to the Scriptures, determined to present myself to God as "a workman who does not need to be ashamed and who correctly handles the word of truth" (2 Timothy 2:15). Only after I had encountered the living Messiah did I begin to search the Scriptures in order to "be prepared to give an answer to everyone who asks [me] to give the reason for the hope that [I] have" (1 Peter 3:15).

I believe that an encounter with God is always a life-changing experience. Such an encounter can spin a person around and send him or her off in a completely new direction.

Consider what happened to Abraham, the patriarch of the Jewish people. Abraham was 75 years old. He had built a good life for himself. He was comfortable and well-to-do. Then he had an encounter with God. Genesis 12:1 says that God told him, " 'Leave your country, your people and your father's household and go to the land I will show you.'" Suddenly Abraham was gathering his belongings, uprooting his family and heading off to a strange land.

Abraham did not question. He simply obeyed. In a sense, that is what happened to me. I never wanted to leave my comfortable, safe, middle-class Jewish world. But then I encountered God, and everything changed dramatically—for the better.

If you are already a believer, I pray that the evidence presented in this book reaffirms your own personal encounter with Yeshua, Jesus of Nazareth, and that it also helps you share your faith in an intelligent way with others you care about. If you are not yet a believer, I hope this book helps move you forward in your spiritual search for truth. And finally, a special request to my Jewish friends who have not yet taken the leap of faith that I have. I encourage you to read this book with an open mind and pray that the God of Abraham, Isaac and Jacob will show you the truth.

—JONATHAN BERNIS
PHOENIX, ARIZONA
APRIL 30, 2010

1

MY SEARCH FOR THE "REAL" JESUS

As a child growing up in a typical American Jewish family, I did not know much about Jesus of Nazareth. I had no idea that He was a Jew or that, like me, He had grown up observing Jewish Holy Days and attending Shabbat services at synagogue. I did not know that He said He had been sent to "the lost sheep of Israel." To me, Jesus was a foreign deity—the god of the Christians. I had no more in common with Him than I had with Buddha, Mohammed, Krishna or any other god.

But there was one thing that made Jesus different. He was an enemy of the Jewish people. I knew that over the centuries many atrocities had been committed against the Jewish people in His name. The Crusades of the Middle Ages. The pogroms of Eastern Europe. Hitler's mass killing of Jews during World War II. I assumed that all of this sprang naturally from what Jesus taught. I was told often, and forcefully, that it was impossible to be a Jew and accept the divinity of Jesus. The minute you did, something happened—snap!—and your Jewishness was gone. Although I was not religious, my Jewish identity was important to me. I was born a Jew and I would die a Jew. And Jews did not believe in Jesus!

WORSHIPING A DISTANT GOD

My family went to synagogue for the High Holy Days, and we celebrated Passover, Hanukkah and the other significant Jewish feasts. I attended classes at the large reformed synagogue, Temple Brith Kodesh in Rochester, New York, and performed my Bar Mitzvah at age thirteen. This was my heritage, but it had little impact on my life, and I never felt that I had any sort of relationship with God.

Growing up, I learned a lot *about* God: how He parted the Red Sea, gave a shepherd named David victory over a mighty giant named Goliath, saved Daniel from the lion's den and so forth. But this "education" was not much different from what I learned in school *about* George Washington and Abraham Lincoln. I knew that George Washington was the first president of the United States and that he often was referred to as "The Father of Our Country." I knew that Abraham Lincoln had freed the slaves. But I never felt that I *knew* Washington or Lincoln. And I certainly did not feel that I *knew* God.

Of course, I had several friends who were Christians, at least culturally. But we never talked about what our families believed. I was born a Jew, just as they were born Christians, and we never talked about it.

Then in high school, one of my wrestling coaches, Dave Toth, was quite open about the fact that he was a committed follower of Jesus. It was clear that something was different about him. He knew why he was here on this earth and where he was going. He had an unusual peace about him. It intrigued me to hear him talk about his faith. I found it compelling that anyone could believe he had such a close, personal relationship with God. But whatever it was that he had, it was not for Jews like me.

After graduating from high school, I headed off to the University of Buffalo. My plan was to complete a degree in business and make as much money as I possibly could. I also planned to have a good time. Like many other students around me during this era, I partied. I experimented with pot and other mind-expanding drugs. I searched in counterculture philosophy, cults and even the occult. Although I partied hard, I was still able to maintain a decent grade point average. That was not true of a friend of mine. Over time, she began to use drugs more and more. School became less important to her. She lost weight. Her appearance became less of a concern. Eventually I lost touch with her.

When I saw her again months later, she was smiling, her eyes sparkled, and she looked neat and clean. "What happened to you?" I asked.

"I've been born again," she said, and I quickly wished I had not asked. She proceeded to tell me in great detail how Jesus had taken away her craving for drugs and given her a new life. When she finally paused long enough for me to get a word in edgewise, my response was typical of those who have a subjective worldview: "I'm happy for you," I said. "This is so great for you—but it is not for me."

Whatever had happened to her had not only changed her life but had also turned her into a persistent and rather annoying evangelist. Over the next week she called me every day, asking questions such as "Do you know why you are here on the earth?" and "Where would you go if you died right now?"

I tried to be forceful with her. "Listen," I said. "I'm glad you have found something that works for you. But it is not for me. So please leave me alone."

But she would not. And despite my protestation that I was "doing just fine," my friend's questions hit me hard. Why *was* I here? Where *would* I go if I died?

She would not let go. My head told me not to answer the phone when she called, but my heart was drawn to these conversations. Eventually she wore me down, and I agreed to go with her to a small home Bible study.

But it was not just the persistence of her witness that got me to go. When she and I were both on drugs, we had spent some time talking about war, violence and hatred—and decided that the end of the world must be near. Now she told me that her group was studying the last days in the book of Revelation. That was the clincher.

From the moment I walked into that basement room in Amherst, New York, I wanted to turn around and run. Clearly this was no place for a Jewish boy—especially one who was still doing drugs. Almost immediately a gentleman in his sixties approached, kissed me on the cheek to welcome me, and asked, "Do you know Jesus?"

Then a second man, the study leader, introduced himself in an unmistakable German accent. Things were getting worse by the minute. I had always been taught that Gentiles did not like Jews. But Germans hated us! I just knew everyone was staring at me. I wanted to leave but could not.

You see, my only mode of transportation was a Suzuki 750 motorcycle. It was a terrible, stormy night, complete with pouring and blowing rain. By the time I had arrived at the Bible study, I had been soaked to the skin. The leader's wife had given me some dry clothes while my own clothes tumbled around in her clothes dryer. I could not leave without my clothes!

The study session seemed to go on for hours, although it was probably only around ninety minutes or so. I was miserable. I felt completely out of place and was positive that everyone there was fully aware of my extreme discomfort.

When the meeting finally ended, the leader came over and asked if I would join him in the living room for a few minutes. What could I do? My clothes were still in the dryer.

I followed him into the living room and sat on the couch, where we were joined by the older gentleman who had kissed me on the cheek. He placed a Bible in my lap and began to lead me through the Scriptures, beginning with Romans 3:23: "For all have sinned and fall short of the glory of God." *Interesting.*

Then he turned to Romans 6:23: "For the wages of sin is death, but the gift of God is eternal life in Christ [Messiah] Jesus our Lord." At that moment I had what I can only refer to as a supernatural experience. While I did not have a vision or hear a heavenly voice, the room became abnormally bright and warm. I began to sweat profusely, and I felt as though that couch had arms that reached out and grabbed me—holding me in place. My experience was so significant that I wondered if perhaps the room had been rigged to produce this amazing response. I even went back later to inspect that couch and the lighting in the room but found nothing irregular about either one.

Suddenly I was keenly aware of my own separation from a God who was real and personal. It was that plain and simple. God was showing me He had a plan for my life that was different from my own, and that He was calling me to follow Him. I struggled with an innate understanding that this direction would mean leaving behind my own goals and ambitions. My heart was ready to respond, but my head was not. In the end, I prayed a prayer with him, asking God to forgive me of my sins and inviting Jesus to come into my life. But to be honest, I prayed more to appease him and end this strange experience than anything else. This is typical of the response I have seen in so many people over the years.

GROWING CLOSER

Over the next few days I started to have this newfound desire to read the Bible. But I did not have a Bible and did not know where to get one. I wanted to read the New Testament in particular, but where does a good Jewish boy go to shop for a New Testament? I could not go to my friends—they were all druggies. I could not go to the rabbi—he surely would not allow me to read the New Testament. I had no idea that the Bible was the bestselling book of all time, and I could have bought one at any grocery store or pharmacy!

Finally I remembered that Dave Toth, the wrestling coach I had admired in high school, had given me a Bible, telling me I would need it someday. I had thrown it into a box in the closet of my room at home and forgotten about it.

I jumped on my motorcycle, drove more than sixty miles to my parents' house, ran up to my room and dug through the box in the closet until I found the Bible. I ran back out of the house without ever telling my parents hello or goodbye and drove back to my dorm room, where I locked the door and began devouring the Scriptures.

I was shocked by much of what I read. I had expected to read about Jesus Christ, the God of Christianity. After all, this was a Christian book. I had not expected to find references to Abraham, Moses, David and the other Jewish heroes I had learned about in Sabbath school as a child. I was amazed to see in a footnote that *Jesus* was an Anglicized version of the Hebrew name *Yeshua* and that the name meant "salvation." My eyes widened in surprise when I read that He had been sent "to the lost sheep of Israel" (Matthew 15:24). I was astounded to learn that His parents were Jews, He was born in Israel, and all of His first followers were Jews. This was so contrary to what I had been taught.

My shock was even greater when I went back to my own Hebrew

Scriptures and discovered prophecy after prophecy that clearly pointed toward Yeshua as the promised Messiah of Israel. I read the Bible for hours at a time, and every word seemed to leap off the page and shoot straight into my heart. Over the next few weeks, as I continued to study the Bible, I began to sense that God had a specific destiny for my life. Ultimately I sensed that He was calling me to full-time ministry in which I would tell my fellow Jews about the One I was now thoroughly convinced was the Savior of the world and the Messiah of Israel. Over the months that followed, a complete and total transformation took place, and I soon switched my major from business to a degree in classics in Jewish studies and early Christianity.

TAKING A STAND

Finally I felt the time had come to tell my parents what had happened to me. If you are Jewish or have close Jewish friends, you already know how they reacted.

They responded with a gamut of emotions—guilt, anger, tears of sorrow. To them I had turned my back on my Jewish heritage. When I told them that what I had done was exactly the opposite, and that I now understood what it meant to be a Jew, they did not get it. They felt they had failed as good Jewish parents because the strongest responsibility of any Jewish parent—or any Jew, really— is the preservation of the Jewish people. In fact, many Jews who do not believe in God do believe in the preservation of the Jewish people. My parents did what any good Jewish parents would. They sent me to the rabbi. But first, my mother wanted me to meet with a "nonsectarian psychologist," as she put it.

As a new believer in the Bible, I now fully accepted the Ten Commandments. As I understood things then, that meant God expected me to honor my mother and father. I had to do what they wanted. So I said I would.

My mom set an appointment with the "nonsectarian counselor" and handed me a note with the time, address and name of the person. When I arrived at the address she gave me, to my surprise, I discovered it was the Jewish Family Services. I spent an hour with the Jewish counselor. She was nice and patient at first, and she listened carefully and with seeming interest—that is until I began to spew out Bible verses at her and assigned her some Messianic prophecies to read before I would agree to meet with her again. By the end of the third session, the counselor was fed up with me. She called my mother in front of me and said she could not do anything more to help me. Hopefully, this was just a phase I was going through and it would pass. Looking back, I know I suffered some rejection for righteousness' sake, but I was also obnoxious. My intense witnessing was just too much for her to handle.

Next, it was on to the rabbi. He obviously was more accustomed to dealing with such situations. He listened to me quote Scriptures, but instead of challenging my interpretation of these passages, he used a tactic with which I was quite familiar: guilt.

"Your grandfather would be rolling over in his grave if he knew you had done this," he said. "He would do anything to stop you."

"But if you would read the New Testament for yourself, you would see . . ."

"Don't you understand what you have done? Just as Adolf Hitler tried to destroy us physically, you are aiding and abetting the enemy by seeking to destroy us spiritually."

Although it was painful, I was not really surprised by the rabbi's reaction to my "betrayal." I have heard Jewish people say, "You cannot be a Jew and believe in Jesus any more than you can be a vegetarian and eat meat." It is not that they are belligerent. Their worldview just does not allow them to see how a Jew can believe in Jesus, given two thousand years of persecution at the hands of "the Church."

Yet it was only when I turned to Yeshua that I discovered I could have an intimate friendship with the Creator of the universe. Now I do not just know *about* Him. I know Him personally. I reached the conclusion more than three decades ago, after an encounter with God—and I have confirmed this conclusion through years of study—that if a person reads the Scriptures with an open mind, he or she will come to see that Jesus of Nazareth is, in fact, the promised Messiah of Israel. And I know my friendship with Yeshua will last for the rest of my life on earth and beyond.

2

JEWISH LIKE ME

As strange as it may sound, I was astounded to discover that Jesus was a Jew. I had no idea. To me, He was a foreign God, the son of Mr. and Mrs. Christ.

My only experience in a Christian church had come when I attended a Roman Catholic mass as a teen. I remember vividly listening to the bells ring, smelling the incense and hearing the priest say that the bread and wine had been transformed into the body and blood of Christ. The whole thing seemed so strange. I thought, *This is cannibalism. We Jews do not believe in drinking blood or eating human flesh.*

I also had been raised to believe that Christ and Christians hated the Jews. *After all,* I thought, *He and His followers had persecuted my people for two thousand years.* I saw no connection between Jews and

Gentiles, or between the Old and New Testaments. A Gentile was a Christian and a Christian was a Gentile. They were synonymous.

When I thought of Jesus at all, I pictured Him as a light-skinned Roman. I imagined a mailbox in front of His house with the address 1 Vatican Lane. I could not picture Jesus as a Jew because I knew a lot of Jewish people, and I never heard of any Jew with the name of Jesus.

YESHUA'S NAME

As I mentioned in the previous chapter, I was surprised to discover that *Jesus* is a translation of the Hebrew word *Yeshua*, which means "salvation." I also subsequently learned that *Christ* comes from the Greek work *Christos*, which means "Anointed One" or "Messiah." The name *Jesus Christ*, therefore, is properly translated into Hebrew as *Yeshua HaMashiach*, or "Yeshua, the Messiah."

Most American parents do not think about what their children's names mean. Most pick a name because they think it sounds nice, or because it is popular. But it is not that way in Judaism, especially in ancient times. Historically in the Bible, Jewish parents chose names that they understood were fitting for their children—names that spoke of their destiny, their heritage or some other important attribute.

The book of Genesis reveals that names are important to God. God tells Abram: "No longer will you be called Abram; your name will be Abraham, for I have made you a father of many nations" (Genesis 17:5). The word *Abraham* literally means "father of many nations."

In verse 15 of the same chapter, God says, "As for Sarai your wife, you are no longer to call her Sarai; her name will be Sarah. I will bless her and will surely give you a son by her. I will bless her so that she will be the mother of nations; kings of peoples will come from her."

The name *Israel* came about in a similar way. After Jacob wrestled with God, the Lord said, "Your name will no longer be Jacob [which in Hebrew literally means "Heel" or, by implication, "Deceiver"], but Israel, because you have struggled with God and with men and have overcome" (Genesis 32:28). *Israel* means "one who has striven with God and has overcome." God renamed him to define his destiny as the father of what would become known as the twelve tribes of Israel.

The son of Jewish parents, Yeshua's name was no different. He was given the name Yeshua because His destiny and purpose was to "save his people from their sins" (Matthew 1:21).

YESHUA'S HERITAGE AND CHILDHOOD

Some may ask, "I will agree with you that Yeshua is a Jewish name. But what else is there about Him that is Jewish?" The answer is *everything.*

He was born to a Jewish couple. His parents were observant Jews who followed the laws and traditions of their forefathers. His father, Joseph, was a descendant of David, the greatest king Israel ever knew (see Matthew 1:16). When Yeshua was an infant, His parents dedicated Him to God in the Temple at Jerusalem and offered sacrifices, according to the Law of Moses (see Luke 2:24).

Although the New Testament has little to say about His early years, we can assume that Yeshua grew up according to the Jewish traditions of the day. He learned carpentry from His father. He attended classes in the local synagogue, where He studied the Torah (the first five books of the Old Testament), the Writings and the Prophets. He most certainly underwent the rite of Bar Mitzvah at the age of twelve or thirteen.

One thing the gospel writers do tell us is that Jesus traveled to Jerusalem for at least some of the pilgrimage feasts (see Luke 2:41–52 and John 7:11–15). I am referring specifically to the three holidays where Jewish men were commanded to come to Jerusalem to worship in the Temple: Passover, Shavuot (Feast of Weeks) and Sukkot (Tabernacles). We know from Luke's account that Jesus and His family worshiped in the Temple that was built by Solomon and rebuilt by the remnant of Judah that returned under Ezra and Nehemiah after the Babylonian captivity. This Temple, the primary place of worship for Judaism, was later destroyed by the Romans in A.D. 70 and has never been rebuilt. These pilgrimages to Jerusalem were a great commitment for Yeshua and His family. The round trip from Nazareth was a 130-mile trek through rugged terrain that took several days.

In Nazareth, life for Yeshua and His family centered around the biblical Jewish calendar. Each Shabbat, the entire family worshiped in the local synagogue (see Mark 6:2), abstained from work and sat down together to a festive Shabbat meal. Joseph, an observant Jew, would recite the traditional prayers—the blessing over the bread and wine, giving thanks to the Lord for His bountiful provision.

Nazareth itself was a small community of a few hundred residents who lived in small, one- to two-room houses built of clay and stone and arranged around a courtyard. Most homes had a dirt floor and little in the way of furniture. People slept on thin, straw mats placed on the floor or, in the hottest months of the year, on the roof. Houses were dark, the only light provided by small lamps fueled by olive oil. Even middle class people had little in the way of possessions—perhaps a pair of sandals, an undergarment, called a tunic, and a robe, or mantle.

By today's standards, it was a poor, primitive way of life. But as the New Testament tells us, Yeshua "did not consider equality with God something to be grasped, but made himself nothing, taking the very nature of a servant, being made in human likeness. And being found in appearance as a man, he humbled himself and became obedient to death—even death on a cross!" (Philippians 2:6–8).

Did the boy Jesus understand His ultimate destiny in life? We have no way of knowing for certain. But we do know He had a hunger for God and a great zeal to learn God's laws.

The gospels tell us that Jesus' public ministry did not begin until age thirty. His childhood experiences helped prepare Him for the fulfillment of His eternal destiny: to lay down His life for the sins of the world.

YESHUA'S FAITH

Although I know it is contrary to today's worldview, I cannot emphasize strongly enough how Jewish the New Testament really is. It is a historical fact that the majority of this Book was written by Jews, Jews who had found their promised Messiah. Keep in mind that all of Yeshua's first followers were Jews: the twelve disciples, the 120 who met in the Upper Room, the three thousand who believed on Shavuot (Pentecost), the five thousand who believed shortly thereafter. None of these Jewish people ever converted to a religion called Christianity. Rather, they were faithful Jews who understood they had found the Messiah promised by the Torah and the Jewish prophets.

A Jewish believer by the name of Joseph Immanuel Landsman was absolutely correct when he wrote:

> The religion of Jesus the Messiah is neither a heathen
> ish nor a newfangled religion. It is the old religion of Moses,
> the prophets and their true and upright followers, but with
> this difference: While the prophets and their followers longed
> and waited for the redemption Messiah would bring to Israel
> and the world, we Hebrew Christians, together with all true

Christians, believe that Messiah has come . . . and that He has brought us and the whole world the salvation of which all the prophets from Moses to Malachi prophesied. The religion of the New Testament, therefore, is the old and pure religion of our nation with the promises He made through the prophets.[1]

In the preface to his outstanding work, *The Life and Times of Jesus the Messiah*, noted Bible scholar Alfred Edersheim, also a Jewish believer from the nineteenth century, writes:

Jesus of Nazareth was a Jew, spoke to and moved among Jews in Palestine, and at a definite period of its history. . . . It is, indeed, most true that Christ spoke not only to the Jews, to Palestine and to that time, but—of which history has given the evidence—to all men and to all times. Still, He spoke first and directly to the Jews.[2]

Through the years many Jewish scholars have recognized Jesus as a Jewish figure. In 1925, one of these, Isaac Joseph Poynser, wrote the following in Yiddish:

Christianity is bone of our bones and flesh of our flesh. The bearers of the Christian message were Jews, and they hailed from Judaism. Christianity was a Jewish movement. We may oppose it on ideological grounds, but we cannot exclude it from Judaism.[3]

I was thrilled by these words from Hyman G. Enelow, who served as rabbi of Temple Emmanuel in New York and as president of the Central Conference of American rabbis:

Who can compute all that Jesus has meant to humanity? The love He has inspired, the good He has engendered, the hope and joy He has kindled—all that is unequaled in human history. Among the great and good that the human race has produced, none has even approached Jesus in universality of appeal and sway. He has become the most fascinating figure in history. In Him is combined what is best and most mysterious and most enchanting in Israel—the eternal people whose child He was.[4]

The great Jewish philosopher and theologian Martin Buber wrote:

We must overcome the superstitious fear which we harbor about the Messianic movement of Jesus, and we must place this movement where it belongs, namely in the spiritual history of Judaism. . . . From my youth onward I have found in Jesus my great brother. . . . My own fraternally open relationship to Him has grown ever stronger and clearer, and today I see Him more strongly and clearly than ever before. I am more than ever certain that a great place belongs to Him in Israel's history of faith and that this place cannot be described by any of the usual categories.[5]

Dr. Jirair Tashjian, a professor at Southern Nazarene University in Bethany, Oklahoma, writes more about the Jewishness of Jesus:

After Jesus began His public ministry, we find Him regularly in the synagogue on the Sabbath. He prayed and worshiped as a Jewish person. The Lord's Prayer that we pray is a thoroughly Jewish prayer. Jesus knew the Hebrew Scriptures. He identified with the ancient prophets. The way He preached and taught, His use of parables and short pithy aphorisms, are all understandable as the teachings of a Jewish rabbi or teacher. . . . It is important that we remember the Jewishness of Jesus. Let's not forget that we as Christians have a Jewish heritage. The apostle Paul reminds us in Romans 9–11 that we Christians must not forget that we have been grafted into Jewish roots.[6]

I love these words from Shaye I. D. Cohen, the Samuel Unger-leider Professor of Judaic Studies at Brown University:

> Was Jesus a Jew? Of course, Jesus was a Jew. He was born of a Jewish mother, in Galilee, a Jewish part of the world. All of his friends, associates, colleagues, disciples . . . were Jews. He regularly worshiped in Jewish communal worship, what we call synagogues. He preached from Jewish text, from the Bible. He celebrated the Jewish festivals. He went on pilgrimage to the Jewish Temple in Jerusalem where He was under the authority of priests. . . . He was born, lived, died, taught as a Jew. This is obvious to any casual reader of the gospel text.[7]

Finally, if you will permit me one more quote, Shalom Ben-Chorin says in his *Journal of Ecumenical Studies*:

> Most portrayers of the life of Jesus neglect to point out that Jesus is in every characteristic a genuinely Jewish char-acter, that a man like Him could have grown only in the soil of Judaism. . . . Jesus is a genuine Jewish personality; all His struggles and works, His bearing and feeling, His speech and silence bear the stamp of a Jewish style, the mark of Jewish idealism, of the best that was and is in Judaism. . . . He was a Jew among Jews; from no other people could a man like Him have come forth, and in no other people could a man like Him work; in no other people could He have found the apostles who believed in Him.[8]

When a rich young ruler asked Yeshua what he had to do to inherit eternal life, Yeshua gave a totally Jewish answer, quoting Deuteronomy 6:4. This verse is known to Jews everywhere as the

Shema: *Shema Yisrael Adonai Eloheinu Adonai Echad* ("Hear, O Israel: the Lord our God, the Lord is One").

He then quoted the verse that follows, also part of this great confession of Judaism, called the *Vea Hafta*: "Love the Lord your God with all your heart and with all your soul and with all your strength. . . ."

Yes, Jesus was a Jew. During His life on earth, this Jewish man taught forcefully and with compassion about the nature and character of the God of Israel, the Kingdom of God and God's requirements for mankind. His teachings are just as relevant and powerful today as they were two thousand years ago. He still touches the hearts of Jews and non-Jews alike who dare to listen to Him—who are brave enough to find out who He was and what He taught, rather than dismissing Him simply as a good man, a prophet or even a heretic. May you come to see and know Him as Yeshua, the Jewish Messiah, who was and still is a Jew.

FINDING JESUS IN THE OLD TESTAMENT

"If Jesus is Messiah, why isn't there anything about Him in the *Tanakh* [Old Testament]?" I have heard this question many times. The answer is that there are many references to Yeshua throughout the Torah, the Prophets and the other Jewish Scriptures. In fact, when I began to read the Bible with an open mind, I was astounded to discover that Yeshua is mentioned more than 152 times within the pages of the Old Testament. The apostle Paul even used the Tanakh to teach about Yeshua:

> They [the leaders of the Jews] arranged to meet Paul on
> a certain day, and came in even larger numbers to the place
> where he was staying. From morning till evening he explained
> and declared to them the kingdom of God and tried to

convince them about Jesus from the Law of Moses and from the Prophets.

—ACTS 28:23

I have already explained that I do not believe it is possible to "reason" oneself into faith. No amount of study—and nothing I say in this chapter—will convince a person that Yeshua is Messiah if he has already made up his mind that it is not true. Once I was like that. I could read the Tanakh without seeing the slightest reference to Jesus of Nazareth. But after He revealed Himself to me and changed my heart with His love, I began to see Him everywhere.

Understanding the Scriptures—both the Old and New Testaments—is a matter of spiritual revelation. As Jesus Himself said, "He who has ears to hear, let him hear" (Mark 4:9). There is a spiritual dynamic that changes the way we see the world and brings the Scriptures to life. Spiritual matters cannot be understood with the head only; they must be seen through the eyes of one's heart.

THE NAME YESHUA IN THE OLD TESTAMENT

Everyone who reads the Scriptures, then, does so through either a lens of faith or a lens of doubt. If one reads the Tanakh with an open mind, he or she will see many references to Yeshua.

Remember, for example, that the name *Yeshua* means "salvation," or "God saves." This name signifies why He came into this world—to rescue us from the penalty we deserve because of our sins.

Let's take a look at just a few of the times Yeshua's name is mentioned in the Old Testament (emphasis added):

"The LORD is my strength and song; he has become my
salvation" (Exodus 15:2). In other words, "He has become my
Yeshua."

"Say to the Daughter of Zion, 'See, your *Savior* comes! See,
his reward is with him, and his recompense accompanies him' "
(Isaiah 62:11). "Your Saviour comes" could easily be translated
as "Yeshua comes" or "Jesus comes."

"I trust in your unfailing love; my heart rejoices in your
salvation [Yeshua]" (Psalm 13:5).

"Oh, that *salvation* [Yeshua] for Israel would come out of
Zion!" (Psalm 14:7).

"May God be gracious to us and bless us and make his face
shine upon us, that your ways may be known on earth, your
salvation [Yeshua] among all nations" (Psalm 67:1–2).

"In that day they will say, 'Surely this is our God; we
trusted in him, and he saved us. This is the LORD, we trusted in
him; let us rejoice and be glad in his *salvation* [Yeshua]' " (Isaiah 25:9).

"I am bringing my righteousness near, it is not far away;
and my *salvation* [Yeshua] will not be delayed. I will grant
salvation [Yeshua] to Zion, my splendor to Israel" (Isaiah
46:13).

Dozens of similar verses throughout the Hebrew Scriptures
mention Yeshua, the salvation of God. You see, Yeshua is not simply
a name in the human sense, such as Jonathan, David or William. It
is much more than that. It is a description of His mission: to bring
salvation to people everywhere.

Still I am often asked, "Well, okay, but why didn't the writers of Scripture tell us plainly, 'The Messiah's name will be Yeshua'?"

My answer is that God does not work that way. Studying His Word is like working on a patchwork quilt. He gives us a piece of the pattern here, another piece there, and so on. The evidence is there, but God does not make it easy for us. We must do our part. He wants us to seek Him wholeheartedly, and when we do, we will find Him (see Deuteronomy 4:29). Ultimately, it comes down to faith.

Furthermore, the name of God is holy. When God called Moses to lead the children of Israel out of Egypt, Moses asked God, "Suppose I go to the Israelites and say to them, 'The God of your fathers has sent me to you,' and they ask me, 'What is his name?' Then what shall I tell them?" God said to Moses, "I AM WHO I AM. This is what you are to say to the Israelites: 'I AM has sent me to you' " (Exodus 3:13–14).

The name of God is a mystery far above human comprehension. It is not to be taken lightly as if it were a common thing. In fact, when the ancient scribes were copying the sacred Scriptures, they often used other terms of reverence for God, in order to keep His name concealed. Even today, ultra-observant Jews will not speak or write the name of God. Instead, they will write G-d. God calls Himself by many other names, all of which reveal His sacred character: El (Mighty One), Elohim (Creator), El Shaddai (Almighty God), Adonai (Lord and Master), El Elyon (Most High God) and many others.

The name of God is so revered that no one is completely certain of the proper pronunciation. According to Jewish tradition, only a few people in every generation know how to pronounce God's holy name. This name, called the Tetragrammaton, consists of four Hebrew letters: Yod (׳), Hay (ה), Vav (ו) and Hay (ה). It is sometimes pronounced as "Yahweh" or "Jehovah," although most versions of the Bible replace it with either LORD or God, in order to be properly reverent.

The Tetragrammaton is considered too sacred for regular conversation or prayer. In his book *Jesus in the Talmud*, Princeton scholar Peter Schafer writes, "According to rabbinic tradition, the tetragrammaton was spoken only once a year by the High Priest in the Holy of Holies during the service on the Day of Atonement."[1] This practice came to an end with the destruction of the Temple in A.D. 70.

No Jew who has any religious background whatsoever will pronounce the name as Yahweh or Jehovah. These names are simply not spoken, out of reverence for the holiness of God, and should not be used when conversing with Jews about spiritual matters. It is far better to use words such as Lord, God or Adonai.

THE THEOPHANY: GOD IN HUMAN FORM

Finite human beings simply cannot understand the greatness or holiness of an infinite Creator. The only way we can even begin to comprehend God is to understand Him in finite terms. This is where the concept of the Messiah comes in. Isaiah 53:1 asks, "Who has believed our message and to whom has the arm of the LORD been revealed?" In the context of this chapter, it is obvious that when Isaiah says "arm of the LORD," he is referring to Messiah. They are one and the same. Numerous passages throughout the Tanakh tell of the mighty acts of this "arm of the LORD."

The Hebrew Scriptures tell of a number of occasions prior to the birth of Jesus where God revealed Himself in human form. Theologians refer to these instances as theophanies. *Theophany* is a Greek word; *theo* means "God," and *phaneia* means "to reveal oneself." Often on these occasions the One who appears is called "the angel of the Lord." Yet He is regarded as God Himself. Most theologians agree that the One who appears in these theophanies is the pre-incarnate Messiah.

The first theophany may be a bit controversial, but it is worth mentioning. In Genesis 14, the patriarch Abraham has a mysterious encounter with a king named Melchizedek:

> Then Melchizedek king of Salem brought out bread and wine. He was priest of God Most High, and he blessed Abram, saying, "Blessed be Abram by God Most High, Creator of heaven and earth. And blessed be God Most High, who delivered your enemies into your hand." Then Abram gave him a tenth of everything.
>
> —GENESIS 14:18–20

In other words, Abram tithes to Melchizedek, which says a great deal about his regard for this man who was both priest and king. Abraham is the paramount character in Judaism—the father of Jewish people. And yet he pays homage to Melchizedek by giving him a tithe. He clearly recognizes that Melchizedek is greater than he is.

Later, the psalmist tells us that Messiah is "a priest forever, in the order of Melchizedek" (Psalm 110:4). While this is a mysterious passage and there are differences of opinion, some Bible scholars believe that Melchizedek was God in human form. In fact, the very name Melchizedek comes from two Hebrew words: *melech,* which means king, and *Ts'dek,* which means righteous or righteousness. Hence, King of Righteousness. The very name indicates he is of divine nature. I believe this is the first Old Testament reference to Yeshua.

The next theophany takes place in Genesis 18, where the "angel of the Lord" appears to Abraham, along with two other angels, to warn the patriarch of His plans to destroy Sodom and

Gomorrah. Abraham clearly understands that one of the men he is talking to is God Himself, for he refers to Him as "the judge of all the earth."

Another appearance of God in human form is found in Genesis 32, where Jacob, the father of the twelve tribes of Israel, wrestles with a stranger all night long. Jacob holds his own in the fight and then asks his foe for a blessing. The Bible tells us:

> Then the man said, "Your name will no longer be Jacob, but Israel, because you have struggled with God and with men and have overcome." Jacob said, "Please tell me your name." But he replied, "Why do you ask my name?" Then he blessed him there. So Jacob called the place Peniel, saying, "It is because I saw God face to face, and yet my life was spared."
> —Genesis 32:28–30

Peniel means "face of God." The meaning of this story is a bit difficult for the modern mind to grasp, but it is clear that Jacob believed he had been face-to-face with God.

Another theophany occurs in Judges 6, when "the angel of the Lord" sits down under an oak tree and has a conversation with Gideon, a man chosen to rescue the Israelites from their oppressors, the Midianites. At first Gideon does not realize who the "angel of the Lord" is. When he discovers the truth, he thinks he is going to die. "But the Lord said to him, 'Peace! Do not be afraid. You are not going to die.' So Gideon built an altar to the Lord there and called it *The Lord Is Peace*" (Judges 6:23–24).

One of the Lord's most dramatic appearances takes place in the book of Daniel, when three Jews are thrown into a super-hot furnace for refusing to worship an idol erected by King Nebuchadnezzar of Babylon. The Bible says that after the men were thrown into the fire,

King Nebuchadnezzar leaped to his feet in amazement and asked his advisors, "Weren't there three men that we tied up and threw into the fire?"

They replied, "Certainly, O king."

He said, "Look! I see four men walking around in the fire, unbound and unharmed, and the fourth looks like a son of the gods." Then Nebuchadnezzar said, "Praise be to the God of Shadrach, Meshach and Abednego, who has sent his angel and rescued his servants!"

—Daniel 3:24–25, 28

Four chapters later, this "son of the gods" makes another appearance, this time in a vision. Daniel writes:

In my vision at night I looked, and there before me was one like a son of man, coming with the clouds of heaven. He approached the Ancient of Days and was led into his presence. He was given authority, glory and sovereign power; all peoples, nations and men of every language worshiped him. His dominion is an everlasting dominion that will not pass away, and his kingdom is one that will never be destroyed.

—Daniel 7:13–14

Yeshua often used the title "Son of Man" when referring to Himself (see Matthew 20:18, 24:30 and 24:44; Mark 10:45 and 14:62; and John 3:13). Obviously this "Son of Man" is divine, or He would not accept the worship of "nations and men of every language."

John 12:41 tells us that the prophet Isaiah saw Yeshua's glory and spoke about Him. And in the ninth chapter of the book that bears Isaiah's name, the prophet talks about a "Son" who will be called "Wonderful Counselor, Mighty God, Everlasting Father, Prince of Peace." No devout Jew, and especially not a prophet like Isaiah, would refer to a mere human being as "Mighty God" or

"Everlasting Father." This language would be blasphemous if it were not true.

Theophanies, then, occurred throughout the Old Testament, perhaps to begin to give human beings a glimpse of God in terms we could understand. If Jesus is indeed God in human form, then it follows that these theophanies were appearances of Him—"the arm of the LORD" revealed. I am convinced that Yeshua HaMaschiach was God, who came to earth in human form so that we might better relate to Him and understand Him.

JESUS AND THE TARGUMS

In the years since I came to believe that Jesus is the Messiah, I have heard from many rabbis who insist that I am misusing Old Testament Scriptures. They tell me I am stretching the meaning of some passages and finding references to a Messiah where they do not really exist. I also have been told that belief in the Messiah was never a central tenet of Judaism. Some make it sound as if the Messiah's arrival was not really that important.

I beg to differ. And Israel's ancient rabbis felt differently. I know this because I have studied their words in the Targums.

The Targums are ancient paraphrases of Old Testament Scriptures. The oldest of them, Targum Onkelas, was completed about sixty years before the birth of Yeshua, and the newest, Targum Pseudo-Jonathan, was finished by the end of the seventh century. The Targums were written because most Jews could no longer understand or read Hebrew. In Yeshua's time, most of them spoke and wrote in Greek or Aramaic.

Here is Micah 5:2 as recorded in Targum Jonathan, which was completed less than a hundred years after Yeshua lived:

And you, O Bethlehem Ephrath, you who were too small
to be numbered among the thousands in the house of Judah,
from you shall come forth before Me the Messiah, to exercise
dominion over Israel, He whose name was mentioned from
before, from the days of creation.[2]

Consider Genesis 3:1, from Targum Pseudo-Jonathan, written
in the late seventh century A.D.:

I will put enmity between you and the woman, and
between the offspring of your sons and the offspring of her
sons; and it shall be that when the sons of the woman observe
the commandments of the Torah, they will direct themselves to
smite you on the head, but when they forsake the commandments of the Torah, you will direct yourself to bite them on the
heel. However, there is a remedy for them, but no remedy for
you. They are destined to make peace in the end, in the days of
the King Messiah.[3]

Here is Genesis 49:10 from Targum Onkelos:

The transmission of dominion shall not cease from the
house of Judah, nor the scribe from his children's children, forever, until the Messiah comes, to whom the Kingdom belongs,
and whom nations shall obey.[4]

And the Babylonian Talmud (completed five hundred years
after Jesus), offers a commentary on Zechariah 12:10. The verse
reads, "They will look on Me, the One they have pierced, and they
will mourn for Him as one mourns for an only child, and grieve
bitterly for Him as one grieves for a firstborn son."
The Targum asks, "What is the cause of the mourning? . . . It is
well according to him who explains that the cause is the slaying of
Messiah, the son of Joseph . . ."[5]

Finally, the Sanhedrin tractate of the Babylonian Talmud goes so far as to suggest that the world was created for the sake of the Messiah.[6] Obviously, belief in the Messiah and expectation of His coming was an important part of the faith of many ancient rabbis and their followers.

THE TRIUNE GOD

Before we discuss more specifically what the Hebrew prophets say about the Messiah, I want to touch on another objection I often hear from my Jewish friends. They start by quoting Deuteronomy 6:4: "Hear, O Israel: The LORD our God, the LORD is one." Then they say, "We Jews believe in one God, but Christians believe in three." Once, I would have agreed with them. But I now understand that Christians believe in one God, reflected in three expressions. Furthermore, I have come to see that the Tanakh supports this belief.

The plural form for Lord, for example, *Adonai*, which is used frequently throughout the Hebrew Scriptures, can be translated literally "my Masters." In addition, the Jewish scribes could have used the singular term, *Eloah*, when they referred to God. Or they could have used another form of the word, *Elohiayim*, which is used for two. Instead, they most often used the plural word, *Elohim*, which refers to three or more.[7]

Furthermore, even though Deuteronomy teaches us that God is one, Genesis 2:24 ensures us that a married man and woman become "one flesh." The use of the Hebrew word for "one" (*echad* or אֶחָד) in this and other passages means "one" in terms of "a plurality in unity" as opposed to *yachid* (יָחִיד), which is "an indivisible one." Those who believe in Yeshua also believe that the Father, Son and Spirit of God are one.

Genesis 1 quotes God as saying, "Let us make man in our image"

(Genesis 1:26). His use of the plural personal pronoun "we" continues after Adam and Eve have fallen into sin. In Genesis 3:22 He says, "The man has now become like one of us, knowing good and evil."

JESUS IN THE GARDEN OF EDEN?

I want to conclude this chapter by sharing one more fascinating reference to the Messiah from the pages of the Old Testament. In Genesis, Adam and Eve hide from God after they "hear Him" walking in the Garden of Eden during the cool of the day. The Bible then records a face-to-face conversation between the first humans and their Lord and even says that God "made garments of skin for [them] and covered them" (Genesis 3:21). (By the way, this is the first instance of blood being shed to deal with the consequences of sin.)

Targum Onkelos, which was completed within the first four centuries after Jesus lived, says that Adam and Eve heard the *Memra* of the Lord walking in the Garden. *Memra*, according to the Jewish Encyclopedia, means "The Word."

It was only when I read the gospel of John for the first time that I understood what this passage is referring to. John 1:1–3 explains,

> In the beginning was the Word, and the Word was with God, and the Word was God. He was with God in the beginning. Through him all things were made; without him nothing was made that has been made.

In verse 14 John explains further, "The Word became flesh and made his dwelling among us. We have seen his glory, the glory of the One and Only, who came from the Father, full of grace and truth." The Word, then, is not just a random statement of some minor aspect of God's character; rather, it is a Person who is one with God yet has His own Being. This Person is Messiah, who walked with God in the Garden of Eden and later came to earth in human form to save His people.

It still amazes me to see how the "puzzle pieces" come together to reveal the face of Jesus. As we discuss the words of the ancient prophets in chapter 4, that picture will become even clearer.

4

WHAT DO THE PROPHETS SAY?

I often hear this objection to Yeshua: "If Jesus is the Messiah, why did the Jews of the first century reject Him?" My answer? Actually, they did not.

Following Yeshua's resurrection and ascension, faith in Him spread across Jerusalem and throughout Israel. In fact, given the lack of mass communication in those days, the rapid spread of New Covenant faith was absolutely miraculous. The Bible tells us that more than three thousand Jewish people accepted Jesus as Messiah on the Day of Pentecost, or Shavuot, when Peter preached the first sermon about Him (see Acts 2:41). After that, the number continued to grow daily (see Acts 2:47). Within months, another five thousand had professed faith in Yeshua HaMaschiach, Jesus the Messiah of Israel. The early Church was made up entirely of Jews and proselytes to Judaism who saw themselves as faithful members of the Jewish community in good standing. It was these Jews who eventually took the Gospel message around the world.

Now it is true that most, but not all, of the leadership of Israel rejected Yeshua and tried to turn the rest of the nation away from Him. But it is important to remember that He came into the world at a time when Israel was under Roman control. Many Jews were looking for a Messiah who would overthrow the oppressors and restore the kingdom of David in all its glory. They did not understand that He was coming to suffer and die for their sins.

We will talk more about this. For now, I will just say that the Jewish people did not reject Jesus because they believed He did not fulfill the Tanakh's prophecies regarding the Messiah. The fact is that He fulfilled more than three hundred of them, and the refusal of some Jews to accept Jesus as Messiah was for other reasons. Furthermore, the remaining prophecies will be fulfilled when He returns in glory.

PROPHECIES OF CRUCIFIXION

Yes, Jesus was rejected by the small gathering of Jews who turned Him over to Pilate and shouted, "Crucify Him! Crucify Him!" (Matthew 27:22–23), as well as a majority of Israel's leadership. But even that was a fulfillment of prophecy, for Isaiah says:

> He was despised and rejected by men,
> a man of sorrows, and familiar with suffering.
> Like one from whom men hide their faces
> he was despised, and we esteemed him not.
> Surely he took up our infirmities
> and carried our sorrows,
> yet we considered him stricken by God,
> smitten by him, and afflicted.

> But he was pierced for our transgressions,
> he was crushed for our iniquities;
> the punishment that brought us peace was upon him,
> and by his wounds we are healed.
> We all, like sheep, have gone astray,
> each of us has turned to his own way;
> and the LORD has laid on him
> the iniquity of us all.
> —ISAIAH 53:3–6

The psalmist also paints a clear picture of what Yeshua was to endure:

> A band of evil men has encircled me,
> they have pierced my hands and my feet. . . .
> people stare and gloat over me.
> They divide my garments among them
> and cast lots for my clothing.
> —PSALM 22:16–18

At one time historians argued over whether victims of crucifixion were nailed to the cross or tied to it. Either way would have resulted in an excruciating death. But recent archeological findings prove that the Romans used large nails to fasten condemned men and women to crosses, so Yeshua's hands and feet would have been pierced. The Roman soldiers, too, cast lots for His garment.

Zechariah also prophesies, "They will look on me, the one they have pierced, and they will mourn for him as one mourns for an only child, and grieve bitterly for him as one grieves for a firstborn son" (Zechariah 12:10). You can read about the fulfillment of these prophecies in Matthew 27.

MORE PROPHECIES

Let's look at some of the other prophecies fulfilled by Yeshua, with the corresponding New Testament references.

- Micah 5:2 prophesies that the Messiah would be born in Bethlehem. The New Testament books of Matthew and Luke agree that this is where Jesus was born (see Matthew 2:1; Luke 2:4–7).

- Isaiah 7:14 says He would be born of a virgin, and the first chapters of Matthew and Luke both say that Mary was a virgin when she gave birth to Jesus (see Matthew 1:23; Luke 1:27–34).

- Isaiah 50:6 says He would be spit upon and beaten. Matthew 26:67 tells us that when Jesus was on trial for His life, "they spit in his face and struck him with their fists. Others slapped him." The New Testament book of Mark gives the same account. "Then some began to spit at him; they blindfolded him, struck him with their fists, and said, 'Prophesy!' " (Mark 14:65).

- Isaiah 53:3 prophesies that Messiah would be rejected by His own, and Psalm 118:22–23 refers to Him as the stone the builders rejected, which then became the capstone. The fulfillment of these prophecies is found in each of the first four books of the New Testament, including Mark 15:9–14, which shows that Jesus did suffer rejection at the hands of His own people. Today, however, billions of people all over the world worship Him as Lord and Master.

- Isaiah 35:5–6 says that Messiah will heal the blind, deaf, lame and dumb. When John the Baptist sent his disciples to ask if Jesus was indeed the Messiah, Jesus told them to go back to John and report what they had seen: "The blind receive sight, the lame walk, those who have leprosy are cured, the deaf hear, the dead are raised, and the good news is preached to the poor" (Luke 7:22).

- According to Isaiah 53:9, He would be buried with the rich. This was fulfilled when Joseph of Arimathea, a rich disciple, went to Pilate and asked for Jesus' body, which he buried in his own new tomb (see Matthew 27:57–60; Mark 15:43–46; John 19:38–42).

- Isaiah 53:12 also prophesies that Messiah will die among criminals, and Luke 23:32–33 tells how this was fulfilled. "Two . . . criminals, were also led out with him to be executed. When they came to the place called the Skull, there they crucified him, along with the criminals—one on his right, the other on his left."

- Psalm 41:9 says He will be betrayed by a friend, and Zechariah 11:12–13 elaborates on this, setting the price for betrayal at thirty pieces of silver. The New Testament describes how Judas Iscariot betrayed Yeshua to the chief priests for thirty silver coins (see Matthew 26:14–16, 47–50).

- Zechariah 9:9 foretells that Messiah would come as a humble king, riding into Jerusalem on a donkey. This was fulfilled in the same week in which Jesus was crucified (see John 12:12–15).

- And, finally, the psalmist prophesies in Psalm 16:10–11 and 49:15 that Messiah will be raised from the dead. We will spend an entire chapter later on talking about how and where this was fulfilled.

Again, these are just a few of the more than three hundred prophecies fulfilled by Jesus of Nazareth. A professor named Peter Stoner calculated the odds of Jesus fulfilling only eight of these prophecies as one out of 10^{17} (a one followed by 17 zeros). To put this into perspective, it would be like covering the entire state of Texas with silver dollars two feet deep, marking one of them and having a blindfolded person pick the marked one at random the first time he tried.[1]

AN AMAZING PROPHECY FROM DANIEL

One of the most remarkable prophecies is found in the book of Daniel (see 9:24–26). I am using the King James Version because I believe it is closest in meaning to the ancient Hebrew:

> Seventy weeks are determined upon thy people and upon thy holy city, to finish the transgression, and to make an end of sins, and to make reconciliation for iniquity, and to bring in everlasting righteousness, and to seal up the vision and prophecy, and to anoint the most Holy. Know therefore and understand, that from the going forth of the commandment to restore and to build Jerusalem unto the Messiah the Prince shall be seven weeks, and threescore and two weeks: the street shall be built again, and the wall, even in troublous times. And after threescore and two weeks shall Messiah be cut off, but not for himself: and the people of the prince that shall come shall destroy the city and the sanctuary; and the end thereof shall be with a flood, and unto the end of the war desolations are determined.

Parts of this passage are difficult to understand, but what I want to point out is that this Old Testament prophecy clearly establishes the timing of Messiah's coming and His mission.

Scholars who have spent years studying this Scripture and the time and context in which it was given have determined that the seventy weeks (or, literally, 70 sevens) Daniel refers to is a period of 490 years. This means that Messiah would be *yikaret,* "cut off," or killed with a sudden and violent end, 483 years after King Artaxerxes issued the decree to rebuild Jerusalem, which occurred in 445 B.C. Obviously, that puts the time frame in the right neighborhood for Jesus of Nazareth to be the Messiah.

But it gets better.

The Jewish calendar is based on the lunar year and contains 360 days, rather than 365. I do not want to bore you with the math, but taking this calendar difference into consideration, the Messiah was to be "cut off" some 476 years after the decree to rebuild Jerusalem—when Yeshua would have been in His early thirties.

In his book *The Coming Prince*, Robert Anderson took the calculations much further. Based on Nehemiah 2:1–10, which says it was the month of Nissan when Artaxerxes issued the decree to rebuild Jerusalem, Anderson calculated that the Messiah was to be "cut off" in the month of Nissan (which corresponds with our modern month of April) of A.D 32.[2]

More importantly, Daniel writes that the Messiah will make His appearance before the destruction of "the city and the sanctuary." This occurred in A.D. 70 when the Romans destroyed Jerusalem and the Temple and scattered the Jewish people in what we know today as the Diaspora.

Note also that Daniel says the Messiah will be cut off "but not for Himself." One of the most likely meanings of this is that He will be killed, but not because He has done anything wrong. This refers back to that passage from Isaiah 53 we discussed earlier in this chapter: "He was wounded for our transgressions, He was bruised for our iniquities: the chastisement of our peace was upon Him; and with His stripes we are healed." We will talk later about Daniel's prophecy, but for now I will just say that according to this amazing prophecy, the Messiah had to come before the Temple was destroyed in A.D. 70. Jesus clearly fulfills this important Messianic prophecy.

WHAT THE TALMUD SAYS ABOUT THE TIMING

The Talmud teaches that the earth will exist for six thousand years (see Sanhedrin 97). The first third of these are the Years of Desolation, which stretch from Adam to Abraham. The second third are the Years of Torah, after which the Messiah will come. The final two thousand years are the Messianic Era—bringing us to the present day. According to the Talmud, the Messiah "should have" arrived about two thousand years ago—at "the midpoint of the world"— exactly the time when Jesus of Nazareth was walking the Judean countryside preaching the Good News of God's Kingdom.

In the eleventh century a French-born rabbi named Rashi (his real name was Shlomo Yitzhaki) completed the first comprehensive commentary on the Talmud, a work that is still highly regarded today. In his commentary, he explained, "After the two thousand years of Torah, it was God's decree that the Messiah would come and the wicked kingdom would come to an end and the subjugation of Israel would be destroyed." He says, however, that because sin was rampant in Israel, "the Messiah has not come to this very day."[3]

Rashi says the Messiah was *supposed* to come but did not. I respectfully disagree. I believe He came as expected but was ultimately rejected by His own people in fulfillment of Bible prophecy. That, however, is changing rapidly as tens of thousands of Jewish people today recognize Him as the promised Messiah of Israel.

YESHUA IS THE EMBODIMENT OF ISRAEL

Another amazing thing about Jesus is that His life so clearly mirrors the history of the nation of Israel. In fact, the entire history of the Jewish people paints a prophetic picture of the Messiah.

I am talking about what theologians refer to as a "typology," a person or event that is a symbol of a person or event to come in the future. When someone in the Tanakh is referred to as a "type" of Messiah, it means that he acted or behaved in a way that represents some particular event in Yeshua's life or a specific character quality He demonstrated. In other words, it is a prophetic picture that is to be repeated later in the life and work of the Messiah.

Hosea 11:1 is an example of such a prophetic picture: "When

Israel was a child, I loved him, and out of Egypt I called my son." This passage obviously refers to the time when God worked through Moses to bring the children of Israel out of slavery in Egypt. But it is again mirrored by Yeshua when He and His family fled to Egypt to escape Herod's murderous wrath (see Matthew 2:13–19).

The writer of Hebrews also touches on typology when he explains, "The law is only a shadow of the good things that are coming—not the realities themselves. For this reason it can never, by the same sacrifices repeated endlessly year after year, make perfect those who draw near to worship" (Hebrews 10:1).

The history of Israel foreshadows the life of Jesus in many ways. At the time of Moses' birth, for example, Pharaoh ordered the slaughter of infant boys in Egypt because he feared the Israelites were becoming too numerous and powerful (see Exodus 1:22). When Yeshua was born, Herod ordered the slaughter of all boys under the age of two in Bethlehem because he feared that the Messiah would grow up to lead a rebellion against him (see Matthew 2:16).

Another example of this foreshadowing occurs when Jacob, the father of the twelve tribes of Israel, went to Egypt to escape death by starvation (see Genesis 46:1–7). As we have already seen, Yeshua and His family fled into Egypt to escape death at the hands of Herod (see Matthew 2:13–14).

Later God brought the Israelites out of slavery in Egypt (see the entire book of Exodus). Matthew tells us that God called Yeshua, Mary and Joseph out of Egypt following Herod's death (see Matthew 2:19–23).

The people of Israel passed through water (the Red Sea) on their way out of Egypt (see Exodus 14:21–22). Yeshua passed through water as He was immersed by John in the Jordan River (see Matthew 3:13–17).

Israel spent forty years in the wilderness (see Numbers 14:34).

Following His baptism, Yeshua was in the wilderness for forty days (see Matthew 4:1–11).

Moses went up a mountain (Mt. Sinai) to receive the Ten Commandments from God (see Exodus 19:1–23:33). Yeshua delivered His most famous sermon from a mountain (the Mount of Olives), during which He pronounced the ten blessings known as the Beatitudes (see Matthew 5–7).

Furthermore, when Moses came down from the mountain after receiving the Ten Commandments, his face was shining with the glory of God (see Exodus 34:29–35). When Yeshua went up on the Mount of Transfiguration, "His face shone like the sun" (Matthew 17:2). In a very real sense, the Messiah was to be the embodiment of the whole nation of Israel. Yeshua's life and ministry clearly fulfilled this pattern.

YESHUA AND THE FEAST OF PASSOVER

The history of Israel reflects the life of Yeshua in many other ways, but here is the most important of them all: When the blood of the Passover lamb was sprinkled on the doorposts of their dwellings in Egypt in obedience to God's command, the angel of death passed over them (see Exodus 12:7–13). When the blood of the Lamb of God, Yeshua, is sprinkled on our hearts, we are spared God's judgment (see 1 Peter 1:18–21; John 1:29). The Messiah, the final Passover sacrifice ever needed, was the perfect embodiment of the Passover lamb. God forbade the Israelites, for instance, to break any of the Passover lamb's bones (see Exodus 12:46). The New Testament tells us that none of Yeshua's bones were broken during His execution, even though soldiers broke the legs of the thieves on each side of Him in order to hasten their deaths (see John 19:31–37). The lamb was to be without defect (see Exodus 12:5), and Hebrews 4:15 says that Jesus was without sin. Some historians say that the Passover lamb was routinely sacrificed about three P.M. This was the same time of day when Yeshua cried out in a loud voice and died (see Matthew 27:45–50).

Yeshua's life and death are mirrored not only in Passover but also in the other six feast days of the Hebrew calendar. Three of these feasts refer to events that occurred during Yeshua's ministry and the other three to events that will take place when He returns.

These holy feast days are understood by some in the Jewish community as *mikrah*, which means "rehearsal" or "recital." Paul tells us in Colossians 2:17 that all of these special days have been appointed by God to reveal the Messiah to the world as part of God's great plan for His creation: "These are a shadow of the things that were to come; the reality, however, is found in [Messiah]."

THE FEAST OF UNLEAVENED BREAD

Let's take a closer look at the other feasts. The Feast of Unleavened Bread began the day after Passover ended and was to last for seven days. Over the years it has gradually been absorbed into Passover. At the beginning of this feast, the woman of the house goes through her home and carefully removes all the leaven. The father and the children then follow with a candle and feather in search of any remaining leaven. Any leaven collected is then taken out of the home and burned. Yeast represents sin or evil. Scripture tells us that a little sin can affect every aspect of a person's life, just as a little yeast affects an entire loaf of bread (see 1 Corinthians 5:6 and Galatians 5:9).

What does this have to do with the Messiah? Plenty. Yeshua is the only human who has ever been without sin. As 2 Corinthians 5:21 says, "God made him who had no sin to be sin for us, so that in him we might become the righteousness of God." Once again, this aspect of Messiah's nature and character is reflected in Isaiah 53. Because He was not corrupted by sin, His body would not decay in the grave. His flesh would not decompose.

The Feast of Unleavened Bread proclaims that the sinless body of Messiah would not experience the ravages of death—and that it is through His sinless nature that we can be spared from the consequences of our own sin. The feast also reminds us that we must yield to Him so that He can purge us of harmful leaven and put our feet on the road to eternal life.

THE FEAST OF FIRST FRUITS

This feast, also called the Omer, is described in Leviticus 23:9–14. When his barley crop was ready for harvest, the farmer would bring his first sheaf to the priest, who would wave it before the Lord. It was a reminder to the Israelites that they were to put God first in every area of their lives.

It was also during this festival that firstborn children and animals were presented to the Lord. This feast points toward who Yeshua is:

- God's firstborn (see Hebrews 1:6)
- "The first to rise from the dead" (Acts 26:23)
- "The firstborn among many brothers" (Romans 8:29)

Another important aspect of this feast is its focus on resurrection. The winter months, when the fields were barren and empty, had passed. Warm weather had returned to the land and new life was appearing everywhere. The barley crop was the first to be harvested each year and foreshadowed the fact that Yeshua would be the first to rise from the dead. As the apostle Paul testified when he was on trial in Rome:

I am saying nothing beyond what the prophets and Moses said would happen—that the [Messiah] would suffer and, as the first to rise from the dead, would proclaim light to his own people and to the Gentiles.

—Acts 26:22–23

SHAVUOT (THE FEAST OF WEEKS/PENTECOST)

Shavuot is the final of the spring feasts. It is also called the Feast of Weeks because God directed that it was to take place seven weeks and one day after the Feast of First Fruits (see Leviticus 23:15–16). On this occasion the Israelites were to bring two loaves of bread containing yeast, which were again to be presented to the Lord as a wave offering. These two loaves of bread foreshadowed the future time when both Jews and Gentiles would become "one new man" in Messiah—when we would be purged of leaven—through the blood of the Lamb.

Paul says:

For he himself is our peace, who has made the two one and has destroyed the barrier [between Gentiles and Jews], the dividing wall of hostility, by abolishing in his flesh the law with its commandments and regulations. His purpose was to create in himself one new man out of the two, thus making peace, and in this one body to reconcile both of them to God through the cross, by which he put to death their hostility.

—Ephesians 2:14–16

Yeshua was crucified during Passover at the very hour the households of Israel were killing their lambs for the Seder. He rose from the dead on the very day the Feast of First Fruits was celebrated. Following that, He spent forty days with His disciples training them for their future ministry. Just before He ascended, He told them to wait in Jerusalem until they had been filled with the Holy Spirit (see Acts 1:1–5).

This was fulfilled ten days later on Shavuot (Pentecost), and there is an important reason for this. Three times a year—at Passover, Shavuot and Sukkot—the men of Israel were commanded to come to Jerusalem to worship God at the Temple. Shavuot was the perfect opportunity to share the Good News about Yeshua with men from many nations, who would then return home and share the news with their families. Acts 2 tells us what happened that great day:

> When the day of Pentecost came, they were all together in one place. Suddenly a sound like the blowing of a violent wind came from heaven and filled the whole house where they were sitting. They saw what seemed to be tongues of fire that separated and came to rest on each of them. All of them were filled with the Holy Spirit and began to speak in other tongues as the Spirit enabled them. Now there were staying in Jerusalem God-fearing Jews from every nation under heaven.
>
> —ACTS 2:1–5

At this point Peter stood up and preached to the crowd, urging them to turn to Yeshua, and three thousand of them did. This was the first great outpouring of the Spirit on the Jewish people, and it is why Shavuot is considered to be the birthday of what has become known as "the Church." Shavuot was also the first of the wheat harvest. Wheat, in Yeshua's parables, represents souls. This feast was the first great harvest of souls into the Kingdom of God. Also, according to the ancient rabbis, it was on Shavuot when Moses received the law at Sinai. Now, it is on the same feast that God chooses for His people to receive His Spirit.

The three feasts we have discussed so far directly correspond to key events during the first coming of Messiah. His death, resurrection and the outpouring of the Holy Spirit are the most significant occurrences related to His redemptive work while on the earth.

After these three feasts, the Jewish religious schedule has a break, and then a second set of celebrations occurs in the fall. Known as the fall feasts, they are directly connected to the return of Messiah and the resulting salvation of Israel.

ROSH HASHANAH

Rosh Hashanah means "head of the year," and it is the Jewish New Year. The term *Rosh Hashanah* is not mentioned in the Scriptures. Originally known as the Feast of Trumpets, this holy day was instituted in Leviticus 23:24–25 and was to take place on the first day of the seventh month. The rabbis moved it to its present status as the start of the New Year based on their teaching that this is when God created the world. Along with Yom Kippur, they are the most important days on the Jewish calendar.

Most Jews are not really sure why the shofar (trumpet) is blown on this particular day, and Leviticus is not clear. But when we read the New Testament, we see clearly how this feast day corresponds with the Messiah's return to earth.

In 1 Thessalonians 4:16–17 we read about the great trumpet (shofar) that will sound in heaven when the dead who are in Messiah will rise from their graves, and those who are still alive will go to meet Him in the air. This event precedes the return of the Messiah, and some believe it will also precede a Great Tribulation. (For more on this, you can read my book *A Rabbi Looks at the Last Days*.)

The book of Revelation also talks about trumpets sounding in heaven as a series of judgments is poured out on the earth. All of this is to prepare the earth for Yeshua's return. It is a warning—a wake-up call that says, "Get ready, for the Messiah is about to return."

Rosh Hashanah is surrounded by a forty-day season of repentance known as *Elul*. On each day of Elul the trumpet is blown to remind the people to repent because Rosh Hashanah is approaching.

I believe we are living in the time of Elul, and God is calling us to repentance. The trumpet is about to sound, signifying our Messiah's soon return. Those who are living for Him long for this day and will see it as a wonderful time of joy and triumph. But those who do not turn to God will experience terror and destruction. We must be prepared. The time is near.

YOM KIPPUR

Yom Kippur is the holiest day of the Jewish Year—a solemn time of acknowledging sins and seeking God's forgiveness and mercy. Translated into English as the "Day of Atonement," Yom Kippur was the only time of year the high priest could enter the Most Holy Place of the Temple to atone for his own sins, as well as for the sins of the entire nation. This was done by sacrificing a bull and a goat and sprinkling the blood of these animals on the mercy seat of the Ark of the Covenant.

Also on this day a scapegoat was brought to the leaders of Israel. They would lay hands on the animal, symbolically placing the sins of the nation on it. Then it was driven into the wilderness, carrying the nation's sins with it.

Why were there two goats? The first one was to atone (pay) for the people's sins. The second was to remove those sins from their presence. The blood of the first goat brought forgiveness. The second goat brought cleansing and righteousness. But only for a short while—and only for unintentional sins. Under the Law of Moses there was no atonement for intentional sins such as lying, stealing or committing adultery. These could be washed away only by the blood of the guilty party. In other words, every sinner had to pay for his misdeeds with his own blood.

In chapter 11 we will talk more about the Jewish concept of atonement for sins and how this changed with the destruction of the Temple in A.D. 70 and the institution of rabbinic Judaism. For our purposes here, I want to emphasize that God's people have never been—and never will be—able to obtain forgiveness without the shedding of blood.

The good news is that we have a Redeemer who exchanged His blood for ours. The debt we owe, for both intentional and unintentional sins, was paid by Yeshua when He died upon the tree. All we have to do is accept His sacrifice on our behalf.

Yom Kippur looks forward to the day prophesied by Isaiah when "the Redeemer will come to Zion" (Isaiah 59:20). Isaiah is anticipating the Yom Kippur to end all Yom Kippurs. On that day the sins of Israel will be forgiven forever, and there will be no further need for the blood of bulls and goats, or a scapegoat. It will be a day of national repentance, when all of Israel will look upon the One they pierced and mourn for Him as if mourning for a firstborn son (see Zechariah 12:10). Yom Kippur will reach its fulfillment when Yeshua is recognized as King of the Jews, King of kings and Lord of lords. Israel longs for this day, and I believe it will come—soon.

SUKKOT

The third and final feast that will see its fulfillment in Messiah's return is Sukkot, otherwise known as the Feast of Tabernacles or the Feast of Booths. Sukkot, which begins five days after Yom Kippur, is a seven-day period during which the children of Israel are to remember their forty-year period of wandering in the wilderness.

Specifically they are to recall how God supplied them with food, water, shelter and guidance. During the week of Sukkot, each Jewish family is to live in a small temporary dwelling made of branches. At night they are to look up at the stars and remember God's promise to Abraham that his descendants would be as numerous as the stars in the heavens. This feast also commemorates the last harvest of the year and looks forward to the day when the elect from all over the world will be gathered into the Kingdom of God (see Matthew 24:31).

There are so many ways this festival points to Yeshua. We will briefly look here at two of them. Just as God gave the Israelites manna to eat in the wilderness, Yeshua is spiritual bread for all who believe in Him. He said:

> I am the bread of life. He who comes to me will never go hungry, and he who believes in me will never be thirsty. . . . Your forefathers ate the manna in the desert, yet they died. But here is the bread that comes down from heaven, which a man may eat and not die. I am the living bread that came down from heaven. If anyone eats of this bread, he will live forever. This bread is my flesh, which I will give for the life of the world.
>
> —JOHN 6:35, 49–51

Furthermore, as His people wandered in the wilderness, God provided them with water from a rock (see Exodus 17:6). Paul says that the Israelites "drank from the spiritual rock that accompanied them, and that rock was [the Messiah]" (1 Corinthians 10:4). Every day during Sukkot a ceremony was carried out during which the high priest and his assistant would pour out water and wine onto the altar of the Temple as the people sang, "With joy you will draw water from the wells of salvation" (Isaiah 12:3). It was most likely during this time that Yeshua stood up and cried out in a loud voice, "If anyone is thirsty, let him come to me and drink. Whoever believes in me, as the Scripture has said, streams of living water will flow from within him" (John 7:37–38).

JESUS DID FULFILL MESSIANIC PROPHECY

I hope this chapter has established that Jesus did in fact fulfill many of the prophecies of the Tanakh that are central to Judaism and Messianic expectation. Some prophecies remain to be fulfilled, but they will be when He returns.

HOW DID JEWISH YESHUA BECOME GENTILE JESUS?

As we saw in the last chapter, Yeshua fulfilled dozens of Messianic prophecies given to us by the Hebrew sages. Many first-century Jews recognized this and became early followers of Yeshua as the Jewish Messiah, while retaining their Jewish identity and continuing to observe practices such as worshiping on Shabbat. How, then, did Yeshua come to be thought of as a blond-haired, blue-eyed Aryan figure—a man Jews do not recognize because He looks so much like a Gentile?

SENT TO THE GENTILES

To understand how this change took place, we first need to see that it was always God's plan for the Messiah to bring the Gentiles into

His Kingdom. Many verses throughout the Tanakh prove that this is true.

In Genesis 12:3, for example, God says to Abraham, "I will bless those who bless you, and whoever curses you I will curse; and all peoples on earth will be blessed through you." This promise to bless the entire world through Abraham's descendants has two meanings.

First, the Jewish people have fulfilled this promise by blessing the world through the advancements they have brought to medicine, science, literature and culture. In fact, although Jews make up only .0025 percent of the world's population, they have won 23 percent of the Nobel Prizes since the award was established in 1901.

Second, and more important, God's promise to Abraham refers to the fact that the Messiah, the Savior of all humankind, would come into the world through God's chosen people. Scriptures referring to this include

> Abraham will surely become a great and powerful nation, and all nations on earth will be blessed through him.
> —GENESIS 18:18

> I, the LORD, have called you in righteousness; I will take hold of your hand. I will keep you and will make you to be a covenant for the people and a light for the Gentiles, to open eyes that are blind, to free captives from prison and to release from the dungeon those who sit in darkness.
> —ISAIAH 42:6–7

> It is too small a thing for you to be my servant to restore the tribes of Jacob and bring back those of Israel I have kept. I will also make you a light for the Gentiles, that you may bring my salvation to the ends of the earth.
> —ISAIAH 49:6

THE MAGI WERE GENTILES

Zoroastrianism was an obscure religion founded by Zoroaster, who is better known as Zarathustra. Zarathustra lived in Persia perhaps a thousand years before the birth of Yeshua. He believed in one God, the Creator, and taught his followers to live good, moral lives. He also told them to keep watch because God was going to send a deliverer who would bring salvation. And watch they did, for years and years, until one night they saw a new star in the sky. Zarathustra's priests were called *magi*.[1]

The New Testament tells us that three "wise men" from the East came to Bethlehem to honor Yeshua shortly after His birth, bringing Him gifts of gold, frankincense and myrrh. Matthew calls them *magi* and says that they stopped in Jerusalem and asked, "Where is the one who has been born king of the Jews? We saw his star in the east and have come to worship him" (Matthew 2:1–2). It is likely that the wise men who followed the star to the stable where Jesus was born were followers of Zarathustra, and thus, obviously Gentiles.

GENTILES IN THE KINGDOM

Even though the Gentile Magi came to honor Yeshua's birth, His ministry while on earth was directed solely to the people of Israel. And for the first thirty years of what later came to be known as Christianity, the community of faith was limited to Jews and proselytes to Judaism. In addition, the Jews who followed Jesus had no idea that this New Covenant faith would include Gentiles. Yes, it was prophesied. Yes, it was part of God's plan. But it was still not clear to the early believers.

Acts 9 and 10 tell us how God began to carry out His plan to reach the Gentiles with the message of salvation through His

Messiah. First, a flash of light so bright it knocked a man to the ground and left him blind for three days. That man was a zealot named Saul who was on his way to Damascus to arrest Jews who dared to profess belief in Yeshua. Saul arose from the ground a changed man, and from that day forward he was called Paul. He quit persecuting believers and began proclaiming boldly that Yeshua was the Messiah. God revealed His plans for Paul in Acts 9:15: "This man is my chosen instrument to carry my name before the Gentiles and their kings and before the people of Israel." Known as "the apostle to the Gentiles," Paul went on to preach about Jesus throughout the known world and wrote 13 of the New Testament's 27 books.

About this time the apostle Peter was praying on the roof of a house when he had a vision of something like a sheet full of animals being let down from heaven. Among them were reptiles and other creatures that no law-abiding Jew would eat. As he saw this vision, Peter heard a voice tell him to eat this food and not to call anything impure that God has made clean. The vision repeated itself three times. While Peter was wondering what it meant, the Spirit told him to go downstairs to greet men who were looking for him. God said, "Do not hesitate to go with them, for I have sent them" (Acts 10:20).

Peter obeyed, and the three men explained that they had been sent by their master, a Roman centurion named Cornelius. "He is a righteous and God-fearing man, who is respected by all the Jewish people," they said. "A holy angel told him to have you come to his house so that he could hear what you have to say" (Acts 10:22). Peter went with the men and heard Cornelius' story for himself. When he did, he said, "I now realize how true it is that God does not show favoritism but accepts men from every nation who fear him and do what is right" (Acts 10:34–35).

The Bible says that while Peter was telling them the Good News of forgiveness of sins through faith in Jesus,

> The Holy Spirit came on all who heard the message. The circumcised believers [Jewish believers] who had come with Peter were astonished that the gift of the Holy Spirit had been poured out even on the Gentiles.
> —ACTS 10:44–45

And that is how Cornelius and the members of his family became the first Gentile followers of Yeshua.

CONTROVERSY BEGINS

Back in Jerusalem, the news of this event caused no small controversy. Acts 11:2–3 says, "So when Peter went up to Jerusalem, the circumcised believers criticized him and said, 'You went into the house of uncircumcised men and ate with them.' " But after Peter told them what had happened, "They had no further objections and praised God, saying, 'So then, God has granted even the Gentiles repentance unto life' " (Acts 11:18).

Sadly, this was not the end of the controversy between Jewish and Gentile believers. Acts 15:1–2 says some men were teaching that unless a man was circumcised he could not be saved, a teaching that Paul and Barnabas sharply disputed. The Jewish followers of Jesus simply did not know what to do with the Gentiles. Their confusion shows that they did not think of themselves as members of a new religion; they considered themselves to be faithful, obedient Jews who accepted Yeshua as their Messiah and believed that they had forgiveness of their sins through faith in Him.

Acts 15 tells of a council that took place in Jerusalem to determine what should be done with the Gentile converts. Some argued that they must be circumcised and obey all the laws of Moses. Others, including Peter, thought differently.

> After much discussion, Peter got up and addressed them: "Brothers, you know that some time ago God made a choice among you that the Gentiles might hear from my lips the message of the gospel and believe. God, who knows the heart, showed that he accepted them by giving the Holy Spirit to them, just as he did to us. He made no distinction between us and them, for he purified their hearts by faith. Now then, why do you try to test God by putting on the necks of the disciples a yoke that neither we nor our fathers have been able to bear? No! We believe it is through the grace of our Lord Jesus that we are saved, just as they are."
>
> —Acts 15:7–11

Ultimately, the council decided to send a letter to the Gentile believers, saying in part:

> It seemed good to the Holy Spirit and to us not to burden you with anything beyond the following requirements: You are to abstain from food sacrificed to idols, from blood, from the meat of strangled animals and from sexual immorality. You will do well to avoid these things.
>
> —Acts 15:28–29

Unfortunately, this was not the end of the tension between Jewish and Gentile believers, or between believing and unbelieving Jews. In Galatians 2, Paul writes about a confrontation he had with Peter because Peter had begun to draw back and separate himself from the Gentiles because he was afraid of "those who belonged to the circumcision group" (verse 12). Other Jews were joining Peter in this hypocrisy. Paul said to Peter:

> We who are Jews by birth and not "Gentile sinners" know
> that a man is not justified by observing the law, but by faith
> in Jesus Christ. So we, too, have put our faith in Christ Jesus
> that we may be justified by faith in Christ and not by observ-
> ing the law, because by observing the law no one will be
> justified.
>
> —GALATIANS 2:15–16

This conflict continued for the first few hundred years after Yeshua, as a number of sects of Jewish believers flourished and then faded. Among these were the Ebionites, who rejected Yeshua's divinity but accepted Him as a prophet and teacher, believing that He encouraged His followers to faithful observance of the Law of Moses. They also rejected the doctrines of the virgin birth and the resurrection, and considered Paul to be a heretic.[2]

Then there were the Nazarenes. These Jewish survivors of the destruction of Jerusalem were active in Syria to the end of the fourth century. Author Philip Schaff says:

> They united the observance of the Mosaic ritual law with
> their belief in the Messiahship and divinity of Jesus, used the
> gospel of Matthew in Hebrew. . . . But they indulged no antipa-
> thy to the apostle Paul. They were, therefore, not heretics, but
> stunted separatist Christians. . . . [W]ishing to be Jews and
> Christians alike, they were neither one nor the other.[3]

Many other groups in Judaism acknowledged in some way the superiority of Yeshua's life and teachings, although most of these have long since disappeared. But never has there been a time of no Jewish believers. In Romans 11:5, Paul writes about the "remnant chosen by grace." This "remnant" is larger today than ever before, and it is growing rapidly.

DIVISION DEEPENS

By the end of the first century after Yeshua's birth, the relationship between Jews who accepted Him as Messiah and those who rejected Him continued to worsen. One of the chief problems for the latter was that Yeshua's followers welcomed Gentiles into their ranks and treated them as equals. This was not something a pious Jew of the first or second century could easily tolerate.

By A.D. 125, the liturgy recited in the synagogue each Shabbat was amended to contain the following prayer: "For the renegades let there be no hope, and may the arrogant kingdom soon be rooted out in our days, and the Nazarenes and the minim perish as in a moment and be blotted out from the book of life and with the righteous may they not be inscribed."[4]

In his book *Y'shua*, Moise Rosen suggests that *minim* is most likely a corruption of *ma'aminum*, which means "believers" and refers to Jewish followers of Yeshua. Rosen writes, "A Jewish Christian could hardly be expected to recite a prayer against himself." He adds that the new prayer was therefore "an effective tool to dissociate Jewish believers from the synagogue. It was not that they decided to leave—they were forced out by the leadership."[5]

Rosen explains further that the final break in the relationship between Jews who accepted Yeshua and those who rejected Him occurred during the revolt against the Emperor Hadrian, early in the second century. The uprising was prompted by the emperor's edict banning circumcision. At first believing Jews joined in the battle, fighting side by side with their non-believing countrymen. But that changed when Rabbi Akiba declared that the Messiah had come in the person of Bar Kochba, the leader of the Jewish forces.

Rosen says, "At that point, the Jewish Christians could no longer support the war carried on under the auspices of 'Messiah' Bar

Kochba. So they once again pulled out. This time it led to the decisive break."[6]

It also led to an almost complete annihilation of the Jews. The nation of Israel was effectively destroyed. Jerusalem was declared off-limits to Jews. Any who dared to enter their holy city were at risk of being put to death by the Roman authorities. Many Jews were sold into slavery throughout the Roman Empire. Many thousands of others fled to escape persecution.

The church in Jerusalem suffered along with the nation at large. Jews who believed in Jesus were still Jews as far as the Romans were concerned, and like all Jews they were banned from the city at penalty of death. By the middle of the second century, the balance of power in the Church had shifted. Gentiles now began to dominate the believing community, and they began to treat unbelieving Jews as enemies of *their* Lord. Anti-Jewish teaching began to emerge, which led to the removal of all things Jewish from the community of believers. The stage had been set for the years of adversity and animosity that would follow.

THE CHURCH TURNS
AGAINST THE JEWS

Before I delve into a deeper discussion of how the Church and Synagogue divided into distinct and separate religious institutions and eventually even became enemies, I first want to make it clear that this conflict has nothing to do with Yeshua (Jesus) or His teachings. Rather, the division came about due to a gross misinterpretation of the New Testament. At its root, it is a demonic strategy to twist the truth and keep the Gospel from reaching those for whom it was originally intended.

During His earthly ministry, Yeshua stated numerous times that His ministry was to His own people—the people of Israel. Nothing that He taught or did was in any way anti-Semitic or against His own people. He came for His own, and although many did follow

Him, it is true for the most part that His own did not receive Him (see John 1:10–11).

Yeshua is the expression of God's will in human form, and Jesus wept over Jerusalem because He loved His land and His people. His heart was an expression of God's love for the Jewish people, for they are "the apple of his eye" (Zechariah 2:8). God's heart for His chosen people Israel is expressed in the heart of Yeshua, and vice versa.

When Yeshua sent His disciples out to heal the sick, raise the dead and preach the Good News of the Kingdom, He told them, "Do not go among the Gentiles or enter any town of the Samaritans. Go rather to the lost sheep of Israel" (Matthew 10:5–6). When a Canaanite woman asked Him to heal her daughter, He said, "I was sent only to the lost sheep of Israel" (Matthew 15:21–28). As any follower of Yeshua would expect, however, when He observed this mother's great faith, He ultimately did heal the little girl. He also said, "O Jerusalem, Jerusalem . . . how often I have longed to gather your children together, as a hen gathers her chicks under her wings, but you were not willing" (Matthew 23:37). It is impossible to read the New Testament without seeing Yeshua's love for His own people.

I am certain that Yeshua is grieved over the terrible things that have been done to the Jewish people in His name. Those who have persecuted the Jewish people over the centuries are not following the teachings of the New Testament in any way, shape or form. Many of them were not Christians at all, but believers need to understand that most Jewish people do not know the difference between those who have a real relationship with Yeshua, i.e., those who have Messiah within them, and those who are merely Christians by name.

THE DETERIORATION OF THE RELATIONSHIP

Let's review the conditions that brought about the separation between the Jewish people and what became Gentile Christianity. First, many early Gentile converts to faith in Yeshua feared being identified with the Jews, since Israel was under the subjugation of Rome and Rome persecuted the Jews. To avoid this persecution, Gentile converts separated themselves from the Jewish people. Although this new faith in Israel's promised Messiah was still practiced within the community of Judaism, new Gentile converts did not want to be seen as converts to Judaism. As these Gentiles assumed leadership positions within what was evolving into the Christian Church, Jewish believers and Jewish practice were marginalized and eventually forbidden. This led to the Church's gradual elimination of all things Jewish, and eventually many Jews fell away from the faith or lost their Jewish identity.

The relationship between early Gentile Christians and the Jewish people deteriorated so quickly that by the year A.D. 306, the Council of Elvira in Spain banned the intermarriage of Christians and Jews.[1] Nineteen years later, after Constantine the Great converted to Christianity, the Council of Nicea convened to seek unity within the Church. No Jewish believers were invited. That was not a surprise, for the attendees issued an edict separating the celebration of Easter from Passover. "We desire, dearest brethren, to separate ourselves from the detestable company of the Jews," they wrote. "How, then, could we follow these Jews, who are almost certainly blinded?"[2]

From there, things grew only worse.

In 367, St. Hilary of Poitiers referred to Jews as a perverse people God had cursed forever. At the same time, St. Ephroem referred to synagogues as "brothels." Within the next decade Emperor

Theodosius the Great permitted the destruction of synagogues, as long as it served a religious purpose. The bishop of Milan immediately reacted by burning a local synagogue to the ground, an act which he described as "pleasing to God."[3]

Then in 415, St. Augustine wrote in *The City of God* that the Christian Church had replaced the Jews as God's chosen people. In fact, Augustine considered unbelieving Jews to be the enemy of God's people, saying that the "true image of the Hebrew" was Judas Iscariot.[4] Augustine came to his conclusion despite the fact that Jeremiah 31:35–37 says:

> He who appoints the sun to shine by day, who decrees the moon and stars to shine by night, who stirs up the sea so that its waves roar—the LORD Almighty is his name: "Only if these decrees vanish from my sight," declares the LORD, "will the descendants of Israel ever cease to be a nation before me.... Only if the heavens above can be measured and the foundations of the earth below be searched out will I reject all the descendants of Israel because of all they have done," declares the LORD.

In this passage God establishes with absolute clarity that the sun would cease to shine, the stars would no longer be seen by night and the waves of the sea would cease to roar before He would reject Israel. Obviously, He has no intention of rejecting them. God does acknowledge in this passage that the people of Israel have done rebellious and sinful things. He says, in essence, "I would certainly have a right to reject the Israelites *because of all they have done,* but I won't do it. Ever." Despite their unfaithfulness and rebellion, God has remained faithful to Israel and will continue to remain faithful based upon the promises of His Word. Furthermore, Paul reiterates the concept of the Jeremiah passage in Romans 11:1 when he asks, "Did God reject his people? By no means!" Augustine's teaching was the beginning of what has come to be known as "Replacement Theology" and opened the door to more than fifteen hundred years of Jewish persecution at the hands of so-called Christians.

SCRIPTURES HAVE BEEN TWISTED

I stated earlier that no teachings of Jesus were in any way anti-Jewish or anti-Semitic. This is true of the New Testament in its entirety. Having said that, I must admit that the New Testament does contain some statements that seem critical of the Jewish people. During Yeshua's judgment, for example, the angry crowd cried, "Let his blood be on us and on our children!" (Matthew 27:25). And Jesus sometimes had harsh words for Jewish leaders, such as: "You belong to your father, the devil" (John 8:44). These statements have been used to fuel the erroneous teaching that God has rejected Israel, or that the Jews are now under His eternal judgment. The intent of these verses has been twisted to fuel anti-Semitism and persecution of the Jewish people over the last two thousand years.

But to understand such verses correctly, one must consider the original context of the New Testament. Gentile leaders within the Church wrongly began to enter into what was originally a "family" squabble between Jews who embraced Yeshua as the Messiah of Israel and the Jewish leadership that rejected Him. Seeds of anger and hatred were sown when Gentile leaders began to take such Scriptures out of context and create an "us versus them" attitude toward the Jewish people as a whole.

The biggest lie that has fueled this terrible legacy is the blame for the murder of Jesus and the labeling of the Jewish people as Christ-killers. So-called Christians began to think of themselves as the new Israel and God's tool of retribution against His enemies, the Jews. Historically, the Christian Church has blamed the Jews for killing Jesus, but the Jews say, "No, it was the Romans."

The Bible is clear about who killed Jesus: No one. He laid down His life freely for us. Yeshua said it this way in John 10:17–18:

> The reason my Father loves Me is that I lay down my
> life. . . . No one takes it from me, but I lay it down of my own
> accord. I have authority to lay it down and authority to take it
> up again. This command I received from my Father.

He died according to prophecy. He became our Passover Lamb, a Lamb led to the slaughter who opened not His mouth, as prophesied in Isaiah 53:7. What killed Jesus was us—our sin—and the need for God to send a sacrifice to atone for that sin.

THE HORROR OF THE CRUSADES

During the Crusades, entire Jewish communities were wiped out and thousands of Jews were killed by "Christian soldiers." Michael Brown writes:

> [In 1096,] Christian mobs in Europe decided to liberate the
> Holy Land from the "infidels," meaning the Muslim Turks. . . .
> [A]s these "Christian" warriors marched through Europe to
> the Holy Land, they marched with a cross at the head of their
> armies. Butchering entire Jewish communities, they claimed to
> do so in the name of Christ. Is it any wonder that when Jewish
> people hear the words *Jesus Christ* and *Christianity,* they cringe
> in horror and run in the opposite direction? . . . Then . . . when
> the Crusaders took Jerusalem, Jews were herded into the great

synagogue and burned alive while the Crusaders, with crosses emblazoned on their uniforms, marched around the building and sang, "Christ, we adore Thee."[5]

This is a sad, sad history that is ultimately the work of Satan himself to try to thwart the plan of God for the salvation of Israel, since their salvation will lead to the redemption of the nations and the return of the Messiah to the earth.

THE SPANISH INQUISITION

The Spanish Inquisition is another particularly dark period in the history of Jewish/Christian relations. Thousands of Jews were burned at the stake during this reign of terror launched by King Ferdinand and Queen Isabella, the same royal couple who supposedly funded Christopher Columbus' voyage to the New World. In fact, in 1492, the same year Columbus reached the shores of the Dominican Republic, all Jews in Spain had their property confiscated and were ordered out of the country. Ironically, some scholars have come to the conclusion that Columbus himself was a Jew who hid his true identity behind the Italian name of Columbus.[6]

During the Inquisition, most of those killed were Jewish "converts" to Roman Catholicism. Coerced into the Church (often by the edge of the sword), they were forbidden to engage in any Jewish celebrations or activities. Many were arrested on such charges as refusing to eat pork or work on Saturday. People were encouraged to spy on and report their neighbors during this time of terror— and many were reported for violations such as not having smoke exiting their chimneys on Saturday. (This meant that they had not gathered wood or lit a fire, which in turn led to the suspicion that they were observing the Sabbath as a day of rest.)

SIXTEEN CENTURIES OF PERSECUTION

Over the past sixteen centuries, there has never been a time when the Jewish people have not been under attack from those who claimed to be believers in Christ. History is filled with atrocities committed against Jews in the name of Christ and Christianity. Here are just a few examples:

1182—Jews were expelled from France, and all their property was confiscated.

1289—The council of Vienna ordered Jews to wear a round patch on their clothing.

1290—Jews were expelled from England.

1347—In Europe, Jews were charged with starting the Black Death by poisoning wells, and thousands were massacred.

1497—Jews were expelled from Portugal.

1826—Pope Leo decreed that Jews were to be confined to ghettos and their property confiscated.

1904—Pope Pius X said, "The Jews have not recognized our Lord; therefore we cannot recognize the Jewish people."

1921—A Vatican spokesman said that the Catholic Church did not wish to assist the Jewish race, "which is permeated with a revolutionary and rebellious spirit."

1925—At a conference in Innsbruck, Austria, Roman Catholic Bishop Sigismund Waitz said Jews were "an alien people" who had corrupted England, France, Italy and America.

1939—Josef Tiso, a Catholic priest, became president of Slovakia and began exporting Jews to Nazi concentration camps. He said, "It is a Christian action to expel the Jews, because it is for the good of the people, which is thus getting rid of its pests."[7]

THE HOLOCAUST

By far the greatest act of hatred and persecution in the history of Jewish/Christian relations—and in fact the history of the world—is the Holocaust. Six million Jews perished during Adolf Hitler's murderous rule from 1933–1945 simply because they were Jews.

A dear friend of mine, Rose Price, a survivor of numerous concentration camps, including Auschwitz, lost her entire family with the exception of one sister in the Holocaust. By the grace of God, Rose is now a Messianic Jew. She told me that when she entered the concentration camps, the guards told her, "We kill you, because you killed our God, Jesus Christ."

These murderous Nazis, of course, were not true believers. Many of them, however, believed that they were devout Christians. And they believed that their demonic theology justified their horrendous actions.

How could civilized people, who actually claimed to be Christians and believed in the Bible, carry out such horrific acts? The answer can be found in the theological foundations for the ultimate acts of Hitler's Final Solution.

Raul Hilberg is one of the world's foremost authorities on the Holocaust. In his riveting book, *The Destruction of the European Jews*, Hilberg writes:

> Since the fourth century after Christ there have been three anti-Jewish policies: [forced] conversion, expulsion,

annihilation. The second appeared as an alternative to the first, and the third emerged as an alternative to the second. . . . [8]

The missionaries of Christianity said in effect: "You have no right to live among us as Jews." The secular ruler who followed proclaimed: "You have no right to live among us." The Nazis at last decreed: "You have no right to live."

The process began with the attempt to drive the Jews into Christianity. The development was continued in order to force the victims into exile. It was finished when the Jews were driven to their deaths. The German Nazis, then, did not discard the past; they built upon it. They did not begin a development; they completed it.[9]

The unbelievable nightmare of the Holocaust was a great tragedy for the entire world. The horror of Nazi rule left a great stain on Christianity.

Many Nazis were spurred on in their hatred even by such Christian heroes as Martin Luther. In his book, *On the Jews and Their Lies*, Luther called the Jews "a miserable, blind and senseless people" and added, "They cannot be God's people, no matter how much they teach, clamor and pray. They do not hear God; so He, in turn, does not hear them."[10] Martin Luther did much to bring about needed reform in the Christian Church, but how do we explain his blind hatred of the Jewish people? It is no wonder that many Jews turn away from the Messiah when they read words such as these from one of the Church's heroes.

ONLY A PARTIAL LOOK

I realize that this discussion of history does not make for pleasant reading. Yet it is only a partial look at some of what Jewish people have suffered over the centuries at the hands of those who claim to be adherents to the teachings of Jesus but are really not true followers of Yeshua. Sadly, most Jewish people have come to equate Jesus with the actions of those who claim to be His followers. As we share Yeshua with our friends, some of whom may be Jewish, it is absolutely vital that we understand their perspective so we can deal sensitively with this issue.

7

A LONG THREAD OF BELIEF

When asked why more Jews do not believe in Jesus, Dr. Michael Brown responds, "Actually, tens of thousands of Jews have believed and do believe in Him. The problem is that most Jews have not bothered to check into the facts about Jesus, and the only Jesus most of them know is either the baby Jesus of Christmas, an emaciated figure hanging on a cross in churches, or the Jesus of the Crusades and the Inquisitions."[1]

Brown's eight reasons why more Jews do not acknowledge Yeshua as their Messiah are paraphrased below:

1. Most Jews have never seriously studied the issue.

2. If most religious Jews learn anything about Jesus in their traditional studies, it is biased and negative.

3. Many so-called Christians have committed atrocities in the name of Jesus.

4. Christians often have put forth a distorted picture of Jesus that bears little resemblance to the real Messiah.

5. Jews who put their faith in Jesus the Messiah often come under great pressure. Some succumb to fear, pressure, intimidation, separation and loneliness, and they deny with their lips what they know to be true in their hearts.

6. Traditional Jewish teaching gives a slanted portrayal of who the Messiah is and what He will do.

7. Once a learned Jew does believe in Yeshua, he is discredited, and so his name is virtually removed from the rolls of history. Brown cites the case of Max Wertheimer, a well-known rabbi of the nineteenth century, whose name was removed from the rolls of his school—Hebrew Union College—after he came to faith in Jesus.

8. Finally, Brown writes:

> Although this may be hard for you [my fellow Jews] to accept, because our leadership rejected Jesus the Messiah when He came, God judged us as a people (just as He judged us as a people for rejecting His Law and His Prophets in previous generations), and as a result, our hearts have become especially hardened toward the concept of Jesus as Messiah.[2]

> If you stop to think about it, isn't it strange that as a people we have almost totally lost sight of the fact that Jesus-Yeshua was one of us, actually the most influential Jew ever to walk the earth? Yet most of us think of Him as if He were some fair-skinned, blue-eyed European. The good news is that Israel's hardening was only partial: There have always been Jews who followed Jesus the Messiah, and in the end, our people will turn back to Him on a national scale.[3]

Dr. Brown is absolutely right.

During the two thousand years since those first Jews put their faith in Messiah, there has never been a time when there were no

Jewish believers. August Neander, one of the preeminent historians of the Christian Church, was one of them. Other Jews who accepted Jesus as Messiah include Michael Solomon Alexander, a former rabbi who became Anglican Bishop of Jerusalem; Alfred Edersheim, a highly respected Bible scholar; Benjamin Disraeli, former prime minister of Great Britain; the famous Lutheran theologian and Hebraist Franz Delitzsch; Jean-Marie Lustiger, Roman Catholic Archbishop of Paris; Edith Stein, who was martyred for her faith; and Israel Zolli, who served as chief rabbi of Rome before coming to faith in Messiah! Many of these men and women paid a great price for their faith.

Let's take a more in-depth look at a few stalwart Jews who accepted Yeshua as their Messiah.

A MAN NAMED ZION

Few know the story of Daniel Zion, who was chief rabbi of Bulgaria during the Holocaust. Zion helped save thousands of Jews from certain death at Nazi hands.

Although he was a pillar in Bulgaria's Jewish community, Rabbi Zion had an unshakeable faith in Yeshua as Messiah and Savior. He never considered himself to be "a Christian"; he considered himself only a Jewish follower of Messiah. He lived a traditional Jewish life. Every Sabbath, he officiated at the morning and evening services at the synagogue in Jaffa, Bulgaria. In between services he met with a group in his home, teaching them about the New Testament and the life of Yeshua.

During World War II, the rabbi had a vision in which Yeshua instructed him to warn Boris, king of Bulgaria, not to bow to Hitler's demand to deport the country's Jews to concentration camps. Zion sent a handwritten letter, which the king received the day before he was to leave for Germany and a meeting with Hitler. King Boris was in no position to say no to Hitler's demands. Yet Zion's influence was so great that that is exactly what the king did—thereby saving thousands of Jewish men, women and children. Zion himself was publicly flogged by the Nazis during their occupation of Bulgaria, but he would never renounce his Jewish identity or his faith in Yeshua as Messiah.

Zion was so well respected in the Jewish community that after the war, in 1954, he was offered the position of judge in Jerusalem's Rabbinic Court—with one caveat. He would have to keep quiet about his faith in Yeshua. Zion could not agree to this and said, "I give up all earthly honor for the sake of Messiah, my mate."

Although the rabbinic court took away his title of "Rabbi," he was still considered a rabbi by the Bulgarian Jews and officiated at a synagogue in Jaffa, Bulgaria, until October 6, 1973. He was ninety years old when he finally retired.

RICHARD WURMBRAND

One well-known Jewish follower of Jesus whom I had the honor of knowing personally during the last years of his life was Richard Wurmbrand. He and his wife, Sabina, had an enormous impact on my life. He always quoted Romans 8:28: "In all things God works for the good of those who love him, who have been called according to his purpose." I have never heard anyone before or after who quoted that verse with such faith and conviction.

Richard Wurmbrand was tortured mercilessly for his faith during the Cold War. A native of Romania, Wurmbrand was imprisoned three times for preaching the Gospel. He spent fourteen years in a cell, including three years in solitary confinement. During this time, the only other human beings he saw were the guards who tortured him.

Wurmbrand was beaten almost daily, often to the point of death.

His torturers would then drag him back to his cell and leave him unattended until his next beating. The savage beatings he endured resulted in many broken bones. He was cut, burned, deprived of sleep, exposed to freezing cold, drenched with ice water and kept in utter darkness and the most unsanitary conditions imaginable.

His tormenters told him he could stop the pain at any time. All he had to do was renounce his faith in Yeshua. He would not do it.

After Wurmbrand was finally released from prison, doctors told him that his survival was a miracle. Underground church leaders convinced him to leave Romania and become a voice for the persecuted Church. He subsequently traveled to Norway, England and then the United States. In May 1966, Americans were shocked when Wurmbrand appeared before Congress and removed his shirt to show his many scars. For many in the West, his appearance was a first glimpse at the brutality of Communist rule. He and Sabina went on to form Voice of the Martyrs, an international organization that helps persecuted believers around the world.

Wurmbrand's life is a remarkable story of faith and courage. And even more remarkable is the fact that Wurmbrand was a Jew who was living a comfortable, ordinary life until an encounter with Yeshua changed everything. Would a man allow himself to be tortured so horribly for an intellectual "belief"? Of course not. Wurmbrand had more than faith. He had a close, personal relationship with Yeshua that sustained and comforted him during those long, difficult days of pain and darkness.

ANOTHER RABBI WHO BELIEVED

During the middle of the nineteenth century, Ephraim ben Joseph Eliakim was an influential rabbi and judge. Husband to the chief rabbi's daughter, Eliakim lived in the city of Tiberias, Israel, on the coast of the Sea of Galilee. Eliakim had such disdain for Christianity that he would not even allow his wife or children to be treated at a church-run hospital, no matter how sick they were.

As he began to read his own Hebrew Scriptures with an open mind, however, Eliakim began to see prophecies that revealed that Yeshua (Jesus) was indeed the promised Messiah of Israel. Eliakim spent hours wrestling with what he was discovering and even more hours talking to his fellow rabbis, asking questions none of them could answer.

Finally, after a long period of study, contemplation and wrestling, Eliakim came to believe in Yeshua as his Messiah. Here was a man who had a leadership position in the Jewish community. After publicly admitting his faith, he was jailed on a trumped-up theft charge. In jail, he was beaten so severely that he never completely recovered.

When he was finally released from jail, he discovered that all of his Jewish friends had renounced him. His wife and children were taken away from him. He spent the rest of his life as a day laborer, working long, difficult hours for little pay. Some who had known him during his former life came and begged him to "return to us and be our father and chief as you were formerly." But, as with Daniel Zion and Richard Wurmbrand, he would not turn his back on his Messiah, the One he now embraced as his Redeemer.

W. M. Christie, a contemporary of Eliakim, wrote of him,

> He never complained. He was content with the simplest of living and clothing, and anything he could spare from his meager resources he used to help the poor whom he met through his continual testimony to the Gospel.[4]

ALL ISRAEL WILL BE SAVED

The prophecies of both the Old and New Testaments are clear regarding what will happen to the Jewish people in the last days: They will come to recognize and know Jesus as their promised Messiah, the One who was prophesied throughout the Hebrew Scriptures. We see a beautiful picture of this in Zechariah 12:10: "They will look on me, the one they have pierced, and they will mourn for him as one mourns for an only child, and grieve bitterly for him as one grieves for a firstborn son."

Zechariah 13:1 says, "On that day a fountain will be opened to the house of David and the inhabitants of Jerusalem, to cleanse them from sin and impurity." This fountain of which Zechariah prophesied is the redemption of the children of Israel through the atonement of Jesus some two thousand years ago. He came for His own, and this is a picture of His own finally receiving Him.

Jeremiah 31:33–34 also speaks of this day:

> "This is the covenant I will make with the house of Israel after that time," declares the LORD. "I will put my law in their minds and write it on their hearts. I will be their God, and they will be my people. No longer will a man teach his neighbor, or a man his brother, saying, 'Know the LORD,' because they will all know me, from the least of them to the greatest," declares the LORD. "For I will forgive their wickedness and will remember their sins no more."

Jeremiah clearly states, "They will all know me, from the least to the greatest." This is a prophetic declaration of the day when all Israel will recognize Yeshua as their Messiah.

Paul repeats this truth in his teaching on the restoration of Israel to the Church of Rome:

> I do not desire, brethren, that you should be ignorant of this mystery, lest you should be wise in your own opinion, that blindness in part has happened to Israel until the fullness of the Gentiles has come in. And so all Israel will be saved.
>
> —ROMANS 11:25–26, NKJV

Again, this is a declaration that the nation (people) of Israel will ultimately see that Yeshua (Jesus) is the Messiah who was promised to them in the Torah, the Prophets and the Writings of the Hebrew Scriptures. I believe that this day is near. In the last three decades, blindness has been falling off the eyes of the Jewish people in greater numbers than ever before. Indeed, it is likely that there are more Jewish people who believe in Jesus as Messiah today than in any time since the first century—and perhaps in even greater numbers today than then.

So what does this mean for believers? Let us go back to Romans 11:11, where Paul states: "Did they stumble so as to fall beyond recovery? Not at all! Rather, because of their transgression, salvation has come to the Gentiles to make Israel envious." Paul is saying that God has not rejected the Jewish people. Rather, through their transgressions salvation has come to the Gentiles to provoke them to jealousy. This is the third time Paul makes it absolutely clear that God is not finished with the Jewish people. I believe this is a direct counter to the teachings of Replacement Theology.

Paul goes on to say, "If their rejection is the reconciliation of the world, what will their acceptance be but life from the dead?" (verse 15). In other words, when Israel (the Jewish people) recognizes Yeshua as the true promised Messiah, Paul tells us it will bring life from the dead. Some Bible commentators understand this to be spiritual life from the dead—in other words, revival. Others believe it means that the physically dead will be resurrected. I think both may be true.

I have studied this Scripture at great length, and I believe what Paul was saying here is that through the restoration or redemption of Israel as a nation we ultimately will experience the restoration of all things back to the time of Adam. It is this event, then, that puts an end to death, sickness and all consequences of the Fall of man in Genesis 3. The ultimate righting of the wrong that took place at the

Fall is corrected with the restoration of the children of Abraham, Isaac and Jacob to their Messiah.

Let me be crystal clear: God's ultimate concern is for the redemption of *all* mankind and the complete restoration of the world. But what Satan understands and has blinded most Christians from seeing over the centuries is that the key to this worldwide redemption and restoration is Israel.

8

IS THE NEW TESTAMENT ANTI-SEMITIC?

She backed away from me as if I had just tried to give her a scorpion. "I do not want anything to do with that book," she snapped, glaring at the small New Testament in my hands.

"Have you ever read it?" I asked.

"I do not need to read it." Her voice shook with anger. "I know what is in there—nothing but lies and hatred toward the Jewish people."

Before I could respond, she turned on her heels and stormed away. I never got a chance to tell her that the New Testament is not a book of hatred against the Jewish people. The New Testament is *for* the Jewish people—written by Jews and for Jews. It is *our* book!

Sadly, many Jews share the views of the young woman who

refused the New Testament I tried to give her. Once I was one of them. A decision was made centuries ago to reject Jesus and the writings of the New Testament, and that error was handed down from generation to generation—eventually from my parents and rabbi to me. I had been taught that the New Testament was full of anti-Semitic language and teachings. Some even insisted that it planted the seeds for the Holocaust.

What an amazing discovery it was for me when I read this remarkable book for the first time and saw how Jewish it really was! I realized quickly that what I had been taught was simply not true. From the first pages of Matthew, where the family tree of Jesus is recorded, a tree that includes Abraham, Isaac, Jacob, David and other heroes of the Jewish faith, *this is a Jewish book.*

I regularly challenge my Jewish brethren to read the New Testament with an open mind—but it often takes a dramatic event to convince them to do it. When they do finally read it, as I did more than thirty years ago, they make a life-changing discovery.

My friend Sid Roth, host of the television program *It's Supernatural,* told me a story years ago that illustrates this point. It grieved Sid that his widowed father did not want to hear anything about Yeshua and, in fact, forbade his son to bring a New Testament into his home.

Sid thought long and hard about how to overcome his dad's resistance. Finally, inspiration hit. While attending his father's synagogue one day, he bought a kosher Jewish Publication Society Old Testament, and asked the rabbi to sign it for him. That night he gave the Bible to his father as a gift. Then, as they were sitting together, Sid said, "Dad, I want to read you something."

He turned to Isaiah 53 and read the entire chapter. When he finished, the old man's face reddened, and he said angrily, "I told you never to bring a New Testament into my home."

"But, Dad," Sid protested, "this is Isaiah 53 from our own

Scriptures." Then he showed his father that he had been reading from a kosher Bible signed by his rabbi.

Sid's dad sat there for a moment or two, looking at that rabbi's signature. Finally he spoke. "I never trusted that rabbi."

Indeed, when it comes to considering the claims of Jesus as Messiah, Jewish attitudes can be deep-rooted. Yet the New Testament—and yes, even Yeshua Himself—is as Jewish as Jewish can be.

THE RABBI WHO CHANGED HIS MIND

In the nineteenth century, a Hungarian rabbi named Yechiel Lichtenstein was among those who hated the New Testament— and Christianity. He said, "Christ Himself was the plague and curse of the Jews, the origin and promoter of our sorrows and persecutions."[1]

The rabbi's anger was stirred by the actions of some who called themselves Christians. But his heart softened when he encountered other followers of Jesus who showed by their words and actions that they loved the Jewish people. The rabbi was so impressed that he decided to read the New Testament for the first time. What he found there amazed him:

> I had thought the New Testament to be impure, a source
> of pride, of selfishness, of hatred, and of the worst kind of
> violence, but as I opened it I felt myself peculiarly and won-
> derfully taken possession of. A sudden glory, a light flashed
> through my soul. I looked for thorns and found roses; I discov-
> ered pearls instead of pebbles; instead of hatred, love; instead
> of vengeance, forgiveness; instead of bondage, freedom; instead
> of pride, humility; conciliation instead of enmity; instead of
> death, life, salvation, resurrection, heavenly treasure. . . . From

every line in the New Testament, from every word, the Jewish spirit streamed forth. . . .[2]

Rabbi Lichtenstein was not a young man when he read the New Testament for the first time. But for the rest of his days he was a dedicated follower of Yeshua.

WRITTEN BY JEWS

Here is a question for you to ask your Jewish friend or neighbor who has dismissed the New Testament out of hand or if you are Jewish and hold this view: *How can the New Testament be anti-Semitic when the vast majority of it was written by Jews?*

The answer: It cannot. The offending passages that some regard as anti-Semitic are really part of an internal family squabble as I previously stated. Yes, some passages in the New Testament can be viewed as anti-Semitic, but only when they are twisted and taken out of context. These passages appear to be anti-Jewish for two reasons.

First, there are and have been Jewish leaders who consider some of the words of Jesus to be harsh pronouncements against the Jewish people. Yet even more passages in the Old Testament could be taken the same way. In the pages of the Old Testament, God speaks to Israel through prophets such as Isaiah, Jeremiah and Ezekiel. Often these prophets and others like them pronounced God's judgment on the Jewish people for their disobedience—and they did not mince words. Was Isaiah being anti-Semitic when he said of Israel, "Everyone is ungodly and wicked, every mouth speaks vileness" (Isaiah 9:17)? Or was Jeremiah sowing seeds of hate when he pronounced, "Like a woman unfaithful to her husband, so you have been unfaithful to me, O house of Israel" (Jeremiah 3:20)? And how about Ezekiel? He wrote, "For the whole house of Israel is hardened and obstinate" (Ezekiel 3:7). Clearly, these three men spoke words that God had given them to spur Israel toward repentance and correction. Why should faithful Jews, who accept as inspired the harsh pronouncements of the prophets, say that similar words from Yeshua are anti-Semitic?

The second reason why some New Testament passages come across as anti-Semitic is that spirited debate has always been a part of Jewish life. As a general rule, when we Jewish people have something to say, we do not hold back. We tend to be honest to a fault. Debating and arguing have always been a part of Jewish learning. If you go to a modern *yeshiva,* a place of religious learning, you will see what we call *pilpul,* a Hebrew term loosely meaning "sharp analysis." It is a method of Talmudic study aimed at clarification of scriptural texts by examining all the arguments pro and con in order to find a logical application of the Law and to sharpen the wits of the students. It may seem that the students are angry with each other—and even yelling—when, in fact, they are simply involved in a spirited debate.

During Bible times, debates were common and even encouraged in formal study. After the morning worship on Shabbat, the men went to a room called the Beit Midrash, where they debated the merits of the sermon they had just heard. Can you imagine this happening on a Sunday morning in the average Christian church? What if, after the final benediction was pronounced, everyone went to one of the classrooms to debate what the pastor had said? It might not be a bad idea. It would certainly keep the pastor on his toes. Yet this uniquely Jewish idea is not likely to take hold in the American church.

Some Christians have the mistaken idea that the Jewish people of Jesus' day were extremely narrow-minded and that anyone who did not toe the line would be punished. The truth is that many different branches of Judaism flourished during the time of Jesus. The Pharisees, Sadducees, Essenes, Zealots and others disagreed with each other. They argued and called one another names, but it was all in the family. The bottom line was that they all were Jews.

Luke 2 describes the time when Jesus was twelve years old and His parents "lost" Him in Jerusalem. The Bible says they "found him in the temple courts, sitting among the teachers, listening to them and asking them questions. Everyone who heard him was amazed at his understanding and his answers" (Luke 2:46–47). Nothing in this passage suggests that the teachers were angry with Jesus for asking too many questions. Rather, they were amazed by His knowledge at such an early age. Being willing to ask questions was not seen as a character flaw; it was a virtue.

PASSAGES VIEWED AS ANTI-SEMITIC

Now let's take a closer look at several New Testament passages viewed by some in the Jewish community to be anti-Semitic.

First, Matthew 27:24–25:

> When Pilate saw that he was getting nowhere, but that instead an uproar was starting, he took water and washed his hands in front of the crowd. "I am innocent of this man's blood," he said. "It is your responsibility!" All the people answered, "Let his blood be on us and on our children!"

Tragically, this passage has been taken out of context to excuse all sorts of evil actions against Jews. It has fueled the fires of anti-Semitism and Replacement Theology for centuries. People have cited this passage to support the idea that God has irrevocably cut off the Jewish people.

But this does not mean that the original intent was anti-Semitic. After all, how many people were in that crowd? A few hundred? A thousand? Regardless of how many were there, they were only a fraction of the eighty thousand or so who lived in Jerusalem—and the estimated five hundred thousand Jews throughout the entire country.

Can you imagine a "crowd," no matter how large, insisting that they speak for all Americans, or all Christians? That would be the height of presumption. The people in the crowd who condemned Jesus spoke on behalf of themselves, not for the entirety of the Jewish community.

In addition, a study of their words indicates that they were not calling down a curse upon themselves and their children, as it seems to our modern understanding. The late Samuel Tobias Lachs, a highly respected Jewish scholar who taught at Bryn Mawr College in Pennsylvania, said that the passage in Matthew "has a Hebraic ring" and cited similar passages in the Talmud. Dr. Lachs explained that the words were a variation of a Hebrew phrase that meant, "His blood will be upon His own head." In other words, "He has brought this upon Himself."[3]

Remember that the Jewish people were sharply divided in their opinions about Jesus. Some rightly accepted Him as the promised Messiah. Just a few days before the confrontation with Pilate, thousands of them had lined the streets, welcoming Him to Jerusalem. As He rode into the city on a donkey, they waved palm branches and shouted "Hosanna!" Thousands of Jewish men, women and children wholeheartedly supported Him. But Jesus also had opponents—particularly many of the Pharisees and Sadducees—who rejected Him and were willing to do whatever it took to destroy Him.

Throughout the history of the Church, it has been a widely promulgated view that the Jews rejected Jesus, and this misperception is maintained to this day. In reality, Yeshua divided the Jewish community. To say unilaterally that the Jews rejected Jesus is simply historically incorrect.

Anyone who is a true follower of Jesus knows that it was not "the Jews" who crucified Him. The Bible is clear that Jews and Gentiles alike put Him on that cross because He died for the sins of all people. This is the fundamental teaching of the New Testament: Jesus took the punishment we all deserved.

In fact, the book of Revelation calls Jesus "the Lamb that was slain from the creation of the world" (Revelation 13:8). Yeshua's sacrificial death was ordained from the beginning of time, so it makes absolutely no sense to blame the Jewish people.

When He preached the first Gospel sermon on Shavuot, Peter said, "This man was handed over to you by God's set purpose and foreknowledge; and you, with the help of wicked men, put him to death by nailing him to the cross" (Acts 2:23). Who were these "wicked men"? The best interpretation of the text here is "those not having the law"—in other words, Gentiles. God's plan for the redemption of mankind through the death of His Son was not executed only by the Jews or by the Romans, but by a collaboration of Jews and Gentiles working together to fulfill God's preordained plan.

There is another possible interpretation of the text in Matthew 27. Although I am not quite sure it is correct, it is still worth mentioning.

The Torah itself says that the life of the flesh is in the blood. Throughout Scripture, blood sacrifice was necessary for redemption (see Leviticus 7:2, 17:11; 2 Chronicles 29:24). When we understand the Torah's foundational truth that blood is required for the forgiveness of sins, we can understand why the atonement of Jesus was so necessary. Blood had to be shed to pay the price for sin, once and for all. When Jesus taught, "I tell you the truth, unless you eat the flesh of the Son of Man and drink his blood, you have no life in you" (John 6:53), He was stressing the importance of accepting fully His atonement through His broken body and shed blood on the cross. It is only through the blood of Messiah that salvation could be obtained.

Here is just a small sampling of what the New Testament has to say about the importance of the blood of Jesus:

> **Romans 5:9:** "Since we have now been justified by his blood, how much more shall we be saved from God's wrath through him!"

> **Ephesians 1:7:** "In him we have redemption through his blood, the forgiveness of sins, in accordance with the riches of God's grace."

> **Colossians 1:19–20:** "For God was pleased to have all his fullness dwell in him, and through him to reconcile to himself all things, whether things on earth or things in heaven, by making peace through his blood, shed on the cross."

> **Hebrews 9:14:** "How much more, then, will the blood of Christ [Messiah], who through the eternal Spirit offered himself unblemished to God, cleanse our consciences from acts that lead to death, so that we may serve the living God!"

In this context, then, it is possible that the people in the crowd were unknowingly claiming their own salvation, their own redemption, by crying out, "His blood be upon us and upon our children!"

ANTI-SEMITISM IN THE GOSPEL OF JOHN?

The gospel of John contains a number of passages viewed by some as anti-Semitic. Two of these are: "For this reason the Jews tried all the harder to kill him [Jesus]" (John 5:18) and "But no one would say anything publicly about him [Jesus] for fear of the Jews" (John 7:13).

When I read the latter verse for the first time, I asked myself, "Who was afraid of the Jews?" The obvious answer is, "Other Jews." Keep in mind that at that time, all of Jesus' followers were Jewish. The Gospel had not yet gone to the Gentiles. In fact, Jesus had specifically told His disciples not to take the Good News beyond the borders of Israel (see Matthew 10:5).

Yet the gospel of John is written primarily for a Gentile (Greek) audience. For this reason, it takes a more philosophical approach than that taken by Matthew, Mark or Luke. John speaks of Jesus, for example, as "The Word" (John 1:1) and the Light that "shines in the darkness" (John 1:5). These concepts spoke directly to the Hellenistic mind.

Because he was writing for non-Jews, John took great care to explain exactly where the events of Jesus' life happened and who was involved. *Judaioi*, the Greek word he used that is translated "Jews," could also be translated "Judeans." I believe John was describing where Jesus' opponents lived, not their ethnicity.

Jesus' arrest, trial and crucifixion all took place in Judea. The high priest, members of the Sanhedrin and other Jewish leaders were from Judea. Take a look at John 7:1: "After this, Jesus went around in Galilee, purposely staying away from Judea because the Jews there were waiting to take his life."

Who lived in Galilee? Jews, of course. Clearly, it was not the Jewish people as a whole who wanted to kill Jesus, but only the "powers that be"—primarily those among the leaders of the Jewish people that were corrupt hypocrites. They were willing to do anything to retain their position and power, and Jesus was a clear threat to their authority. Furthermore, Jesus did not fit their Messianic expectation of the day. So in all fairness, their rejection of

Jesus likely came from a combination of corruption and a wrong expectation of who the Messiah would look like and what He would accomplish.

I love the way Stephen Pacht puts it:

> [S]ince both sides were Jews, neither of them was anti-Jewish. We might liken the situation to American or British history. No one would say that the Confederate struggle against the Union was anti-American, or that the Civil War fought by Oliver Cromwell against King Charles was anti-British. So the battle between Jesus and His followers and the religious rulers of that day was akin to a civil war. . . . What to the outsider might appear as anti-Semitic writing in the New Testament is nothing more than the description of a 'family dispute.' It was a struggle between Jesus, the Jew from Galilee, and the pretentious Jewish religious leaders of Judea.[4]

HARSH WORDS FOR THE PHARISEES

Another text often viewed as anti-Semitic is found in Matthew 23:

> Woe to you, teachers of the law and Pharisees, you hypocrites! You shut the kingdom of heaven in men's faces. You yourselves do not enter, nor will you let those enter who are trying to.
>
> Woe to you, teachers of the law and Pharisees, you hypocrites! You travel over land and sea to win a single convert, and when he becomes one, you make him twice as much a son of hell as you are. . . .
>
> Woe to you, teachers of the law and Pharisees, you hypocrites! You clean the outside of the cup and dish, but inside they are full of greed and self-indulgence. . . .
>
> Woe to you, teachers of the law and Pharisees, you hypocrites! You are like whitewashed tombs, which look beautiful

on the outside but on the inside are full of dead men's bones and everything unclean. In the same way, on the outside you appear to people as righteous but on the inside you are full of hypocrisy and wickedness. . . .

You snakes! You brood of vipers! How will you escape being condemned to hell?

—MATTHEW 23:13–15, 25, 27–28, 33

Talk about telling it straight! These are some harsh words that Jesus directed toward the Pharisees. But interestingly, the Pharisees were the sect closest to Yeshua in their beliefs and practices. They did their best to follow the Torah. They worshiped often in the Temple. They celebrated the feasts and festivals. Many strove to live honest, pure lives that honored God.

The Sadduccees, on the other hand, were the secular humanists of their day. They were more corrupt and collaborated with their Roman captors. They believed in God's existence, but they did not believe in a future reward or judgment, so it did not matter how they lived. Strangely, Jesus did not have much to say about them, except when they tried to trip Him up with a question about the resurrection (see Mark 12:18–27).

Why did Jesus vent so much of His anger on the Pharisees, who were more closely aligned with the truth? Probably because they were the spiritual guardians of the faith and more was expected of them. The Bible tells us that the true teachers of the Word are worthy of double honor (see 1 Timothy 5:17), but stricter judgment as well (see James 3:1). The Pharisees were the people who should have recognized Yeshua as the promised Messiah.

It is also important to consider the situation in which Jesus delivered His stinging rebuke to the Pharisees. For three years He had done everything He could to penetrate their hearts with the light of the Gospel. He had passionately preached the Good News that God's Kingdom was near. He had healed their sick. He had performed many signs and wonders. Yet after all this so many of them rejected Him.

Not all Pharisees rejected Jesus, however. Nicodemus, a Pharisee and member of the Jewish ruling council, clearly was drawn by His teachings and came to Him by night with a sincere and open heart (see John 3; 7:49–51; 19:38–40). And Joseph of Arimathea, also a prominent member of the council, provided the tomb in which the body of Yeshua was laid (see Matthew 27:56–58; Mark 15:42–44; Luke 23:50–52; John 19:37–39). Then there was Gamaliel, a Pharisee, member of the Sanhedrin and teacher of the Law, who wisely discerned that Jesus might in fact be from God (see Acts 5:33–39). I expect to see these three men in heaven among the righteous Jewish leaders of faith.

WAS PAUL ANTI-SEMITIC?

Another text I want to look at is a difficult passage and one that seems out of character for the apostle Paul:

> For you, brothers, became imitators of God's churches
> in Judea, which are in Christ [Messiah] Jesus: You suffered
> from your own countrymen the same things those churches
> suffered from the Jews, who killed the Lord Jesus and the
> prophets and also drove us out. They displease God and are
> hostile to all men in their effort to keep us from speaking to
> the Gentiles so that they may be saved. In this way they always
> heap up their sins to the limit. The wrath of God has come
> upon them at last.
>
> —1 THESSALONIANS 2:14–16

The first thing to note is that Paul is writing to encourage the Thessalonians, who have been persecuted for their faith by their fellow Greeks. He wants to let them know that they are not alone in their suffering and that the same sort of persecution has also come upon believers in Judea.

A second important point is grammatical. Some scholars suggest that the biggest problem with this passage is the mistaken addition of a comma. That single punctuation mark after the word "Jews" seems to imply that *all* the Jews killed Jesus and the prophets. Remove the comma and it becomes clear that Paul is talking about only those Jews who actively took part in the death of Yeshua and the persecution of the early followers of the faith.

Third, remember that before his dramatic revelation on the road to Damascus, Paul was one of the foremost persecutors of The Way. He understood this mindset. Having believed it himself initially, he knew he had been misguided, and so he calls those who continued to persecute followers of Messiah misguided as well.

Another view of this passage comes from David Stern, editor of the *Complete Jewish Bible*.[5] He says that one of Paul's intentions is actually to prevent, rather than stir up, anti-Semitism. More specifically, Stern points to the final sentence, "The wrath of God has come upon them at last." This is a subtle reminder that it is never up to us to take vengeance on our enemies. Rather, we must leave them in God's hands and let Him deal with them as He will.

Now I come to the most important reason why I do not believe this passage is anti-Semitic. Throughout his writings, Paul expresses his great love and burden for his fellow Jews. To interpret any of his writings as anti-Semitic would be to interpret them in a way that would stand in sharp contrast to everything else he wrote.

Many passages profess Paul's love for his fellow Jews (see, for example, Romans 1:16; 3:1–4; 9:2–4; 11:1, 13–15, 17–18, 28–29; 15:27). He longed for them to come into the salvation that he knew to be true and had experienced so radically. Even though he was the appointed apostle to the Gentiles, everywhere he went Paul taught first in the synagogue to proclaim the Gospel to the very people who persecuted and ostracized him. They stoned him, beat him and left him for dead. Still, he said that he would give up his own eternity for them (see Romans 9:1–4). Yes, with the knowledge Paul had of the riches of heaven and the torments of hell, he said he would give up his place in heaven for the salvation of his own brethren. In light of this, how could anyone accuse this man of being anti-Semitic?

THE SYNAGOGUE OF SATAN?

I want to examine one final Scripture used to fuel the fires of Christian anti-Semitism. It is one of my least favorite passages in the Bible.

> I will make those who are of the synagogue of Satan, who claim to be Jews though they are not, but are liars—I will make them come and fall down at your feet and acknowledge that I have loved you.
> —REVELATION 3:9

This Scripture seems to be calling all Jews "the synagogue of Satan." I do not believe this is the case.

There are two viable explanations for what this passage is talking about. First, by the time this verse was written, animosity between non-believing Jews and followers of Yeshua had reached a fever pitch. Martyrdom of believers had begun, and the book of Revelation was written to encourage them to stay strong in the faith, to let them know that victory was coming.

In his classic book, *Letters to the Seven Churches*, William Barclay wrote:

> Nero was the first persecutor of the Christians. His favorite actor, Aliturus, and his infamous harlot, Empress Poppaea, were both Jewish proselytes, and there is hardly any doubt that it was their slanderous and perverted information which turned Nero against the Christians.[6]

From this and other sources, it seems clear that some Jews were responsible for, or at least encouraged, the persecution of believers that took place under Nero. This is a historical fact, and a historical fact is not slander. One cannot rewrite history to make a particular group look better than they were.

Revelation 3:9, then, refers specifically to these Jews, and not to *all* Jews. John was writing about a specific group of people living at a specific place and time.

A second possible explanation of this passage in Revelation involves a different approach to the text. By this time, not only had the persecution of believers begun, but the process of separating Christianity from its roots had also started. Anti-Jewish theology had begun to appear and to attack the Jewish roots of the faith. This theology comprised the idea that a new people, the Church, had replaced the Jewish people, who then came under God's eternal judgment. The assertion of this "Replacement Theology" was that Christians had become the new people of God and that all the blessings of Israel now belonged to them, while the curses were left to the Jews. John, himself a Jewish believer, possibly was attacking the group of Gentile leaders who claimed they had replaced Israel, and perhaps they were the people to whom John referred as the "synagogue of Satan."

Regardless of which explanation is correct, to indict all Jewish people as the "synagogue of Satan" cannot be possible in light of all the Scriptures in the New Testament that repeatedly reaffirm God's love and faithfulness to the children of Abraham, Isaac and Jacob. Not to mention the fact that all the first believers of Yeshua were themselves Jews and were responsible for taking the Gospel throughout the known world.

CHRISTIANITY: THE SOURCE OF ALL THINGS ANTI-SEMITIC?

Before we move on to the next chapter, I want to say a few more words about my Jewish brethren who insist that Christianity is the source of all anti-Semitic evil in the world. While I understand that the two-thousand-year legacy of hatred in the name of Christ and Christianity goes deep into our history and psyche, this attitude is patently false and frankly ridiculous.

Today the state of Israel has no better friends than evangelical Christians in America and worldwide. The nations with a Judeo-Christian heritage have always welcomed the Jewish people with open arms: the United States, Canada, England, France. In fact, it was a believing Christian who paved the way for the modern state of Israel. Arthur Balfour, Britain's foreign minister during World War I, issued the proclamation calling for the establishment of a Jewish homeland in Palestine. Balfour was motivated by his belief in the Bible as the Word of God. He understood that the Jewish people had not been forgotten by God and had been given the eternal promise of a homeland.

A common question we Jews often ask is, "But what about Christians such as Hitler?"

Adolf Hitler most assuredly was *not* Christian. Historian Paul Johnson writes that despite his public pronouncements of faith, Hitler hated Christianity "with a passion" and told members of his inner circle that he planned "to stamp out Christianity root and branch."[7] While Hitler used "Christian" language to stir up the fears of the German people, he twisted Yeshua's teachings in the most cynical way.

I do not deny that millions of Jews have suffered terribly at the hands of those who called themselves "Christians." I could write an entire series of books on the subject. For anyone who wants to know more about this tragic subject, I suggest Michael Brown's heartbreaking book, *Our Hands Are Stained With Blood.*[8] Yet despite the many deplorable acts committed against Jews by so-called Christians, true believers such as Corrie ten Boom and Oskar Schindler, who risked their lives to help Jews during the Holocaust, have always reached out their hands to their Jewish brothers.

At the Holocaust Memorial in Jerusalem, Yad Vashem, rows and rows of carob trees represent individual righteous Gentiles who risked or gave their lives to help the Jewish people during the tragic years of the Holocaust. They serve as a visible reminder that there were and are true Christians who love the Jewish people even at the cost of their own lives.

It is also important to remember that anti-Semitism did not start with the Christian Church. Jews were enslaved in Egypt. Their baby boys were slaughtered. In Persia, a jealous government official named Haman plotted to kill the Jews, until God appointed Queen Esther to save her people. In fact, anti-Semitism has existed since God called Abram to be the father of the Jewish people. So anti-Semitism is not a purely Christian phenomenon.

MISUSE OF SCRIPTURE ON BOTH SIDES IS WRONG

To summarize, although it is true that Yeshua and other authors of the New Testament made critical statements against the Jewish leadership and those who were opposing and persecuting the faith, this was, in fact, an in-house struggle—a family feud. To move any New Testament Scripture out of that context is patently wrong.

Furthermore, for Gentile Christians to use these Scriptures against the Jewish people is evil and grieves the heart of God, who remains faithful to the Jewish people and longs for their return to Him through His Son, Yeshua, the Messiah of Israel.

FINDING JESUS IN HISTORY

Now and then I run into someone who insists, "Jesus never existed. He is just a myth—like Zeus or Hercules."

Twenty years ago I used to hear this argument much more frequently than I do today. Archeological discoveries have increased our knowledge of history to the point that denying Jesus lived is like denying that Abraham Lincoln or George Washington existed. Plenty of evidence proves that Jesus walked the dusty roads of Israel two thousand years ago.

Yet even if the extra-biblical evidence for Jesus did not exist, the Bible has proven to be reliable over and over again. The more we know, the more we see that the accuracy of the Bible has endured the scrutiny of history.

ARCHEOLOGICAL TRUTH FOUND IN THE BIBLE

I have a special interest in archeology and had the privilege of studying the subject on an excavation in Israel for a semester as part of
my undergraduate degree. Because of this, I do my best to keep
up with the latest archeological news from Israel and the Middle
East. Over and over again, the Bible is used within the archeological
community—and is proven accurate in its description of events,
places and people. Let's examine some of the archeological evidence
that supports the truth of the Bible:[1]

Abraham Was Real

Critics once said that Abraham was a fictional character "invented"
by later generations of Jewish people to explain the origins of our
people. Then his name was found inscribed on the walls of a temple
erected in Egypt by Pharaoh Shishak—who is believed to be identi-
cal to Ramses II.

The Fall of Jericho Was Accurate

Critics have also disputed the Bible's account of the fall of Jericho. The
book of Joshua says the walls of the city collapsed when the Israelites
marched around them, blew their trumpets and shouted (see Joshua
6:20–21). "City walls simply do not fall down like that," some scoffed.
Then an excavation from 1952–58 conducted by Kathleen Kenyon, a
leading British archeologist of neolithic culture in the Fertile Crescent,
discovered that Jericho's walls had, indeed, fallen outward, rather than
inward, as one would expect from an all-out military assault.

Luke Was a Trustworthy Historian

Skeptics also have had to admit that New Testament writers knew
what they were talking about. For years, secular historians were

especially hard on Luke, who wrote the gospel bearing his name, as well as the book of Acts. Here are just a few examples of criticisms that have since been refuted:

- Historians said Luke was wrong when he called Philippi a "district" of Macedonia (see Acts 16:12). Then archeologists found inscriptions that confirmed this.

- Luke was criticized for using the term *politarchs* to describe authorities in the Greek city of Thessalonica (see Acts 17:6). In recent years, nineteen inscriptions have been found that use this word, and five refer directly to Thessalonica.

- Historians also questioned Luke's use of the term *proconsul* as the title for Gallio (see Acts 18:12). Then an inscription dated from A.D. 52 was unearthed, which says, "As Lucius Annaeus Gallio, my friend and the proconsul of Achaia. . . ."

Obviously, Luke was meticulous in his research and use of facts. It seems to me that if we can trust the first-century doctor with minor details like these, we can certainly trust him when he records his version of the Gospel. While Luke was not there in person to hear the teachings or to witness the miracles Jesus performed, he was obviously well acquainted with Paul. He knew Paul's integrity and had a front-row seat to the apostle's amazing, miracle-filled life. He witnessed, for example, God's power when Paul, after being shipwrecked, was bitten by a poisonous snake but suffered no effects. He also witnessed Paul heal the father of Publius, chief official of the island, and then many other sick people (see Acts 28:3–9). Because we can trust Luke's attention to detail, we can also trust his representation of facts.

As archeologist and Oxford professor Sir William Mitchell Ramsay notes, "Luke is a historian of the first rank; not merely are his statements of fact trustworthy . . . but [he] also should be placed along with the very greatest of historians."[2]

Author and historian Dr. Norman L. Geisler agrees: "In all, Luke names 32 countries, 54 cities and nine islands without a [factual or historical] error."[3]

The fact that Luke and the other biblical writers were so meticulous about their facts shows just how trustworthy they were. They were not content to report hearsay or "urban legends." They were reporters, not storytellers.

ARCHEOLOGY CONTINUES TO CONFIRM THE BIBLE

In his bestselling book, *Evidence That Demands a Verdict*, Josh McDowell quotes a number of archeological experts regarding the historical reliability of the New Testament. He quotes Yale University's Millard Burrows: "Archeology has in many cases refuted the views of modern critics [of the New Testament]. It has shown in a number of instances that these views rest on false assumptions and unreal, artificial schemes of historical development."[4]

Merrill Unger, author of *Archeology and the New Testament*, is also quoted: "The role which archeology is performing in New Testament research (as well as that of the Old Testament) in expediting scientific study, balancing critical theory, illustrating, elucidating, supplementing, and authenticating historical and cultural backgrounds, constitutes the one bright spot in the future of the sacred text."[5]

F. F. Bruce adds: "It may be legitimate to say that archeology has confirmed the New Testament record."[6]

EXTRA-BIBLICAL REFERENCES TO JESUS

As I mentioned, the Bible is not the only place we find references to Jesus. Many other historical, nonreligious sources contain references to Jesus and His followers.

The Talmud

The Talmud contains references to Yeshua and His early followers, although as one would expect, they do not necessarily picture Him in an altogether positive light.

> On (Sabbath eve and) the eve of Passover, Jesus the Nazarene was hanged. . . . Since they did not find anything in his defense, they hanged him on (Sabbath eve and) the eve of Passover.[7]

This passage is obviously written from the point of view of Yeshua's enemies, but it is strong evidence that He existed and that He was executed at the beginning of Passover, just as the Bible says.

Another passage from the Talmud shows that even Jewish people who did not accept Yeshua as Messiah believed that His followers could heal disease—though they did not attribute this power to God. The passage reads:

> No man should have any dealings with *Minim* [Jewish followers of Jesus who were now banned from synagogue attendance], nor is it allowed to be healed by them. . . . It is different with the teaching of *Minim,* for it draws and one [having dealings with them] may be drawn after them.[8]

While they were instructing Jews not to be healed by followers of Yeshua, their instruction clearly proves their belief in the reality of these healings. Incidentally, this was not the first time Jesus' critics accused Him of healing through ungodly means. Mark 3 tells of the time when some teachers of the Law accused Him of driving out demons by the power of Beelzebub, the prince of demons. Jesus responded,

How can Satan drive out Satan? If a kingdom is divided against itself, that kingdom cannot stand. If a house is divided against itself, that house cannot stand. And if Satan opposes himself and is divided, he cannot stand; his end has come.

—MARK 3:23–26

Flavius Josephus

A Jewish historian born in Jerusalem in A.D. 37, Flavius Josephus served as commander of Jewish forces in Galilee prior to being captured by the Romans. His writing, perhaps the most important literary source material of that time, further supports the existence of Jesus.

Admittedly, some historians dispute the first passage below. They agree that much of the passage is authentic but believe it was "embellished" by a later Christian editor. I have placed the disputed portions of this passage in brackets. Remember that we are not looking for literary support of Yeshua's resurrection or His claims to be the Messiah, but rather for historical evidence that acknowledges His existence:

Now, there was about this time Jesus, a wise man, [if it be lawful to call him a man,] for he was a doer of wonderful works, a teacher of such men as receive the truth with pleasure. He drew over to him both many of the Jews and many of the Gentiles. [He was the Christ] and when Pilate, at the suggestion of the principal men among us, had condemned him to the cross, those that loved him at the first did not forsake him [for he appeared to them alive again on the third day; as the divine prophets had foretold and three and ten thousand other wonderful things concerning him.] And the tribe of Christians so named for him are not extinct at this day.[9]

According to Josephus expert Louis H. Feldman, the authenticity of the second passage (below) "has been almost universally acknowledged" by scholars.

> But the younger Ananus who, as we said, received the high priesthood, was of a bold disposition and exceptionally daring; he followed the party of the Sadducees, who are severe in judgment above all the Jews, as we have already shown. As therefore Ananus was of such a disposition, he thought he had now a good opportunity, as Festus was now dead, and Albinus was still on the road; so he assembled a council of judges, and brought before it the brother of Jesus the so-called Christ, whose name was James, together with some others, and having accused them as lawbreakers, he delivered them over to be stoned ([Feldman is quoting Josephus'] *Jewish Antiquities* 20.9.1).[10]

Mara Bar Sarapion

Another historical reference is from Mara Bar Sarapion, a Syrian philosopher, whom many believe provided one of the earliest non-Jewish, non-Christian references to Jesus. He wrote the following letter to his son to encourage him in the pursuit of wisdom and knowledge. We do not know the exact date the letter was written, although it was shortly after the destruction of Jerusalem in A.D. 70.

> What are we to say when the wise are forcibly dragged by the hands of tyrants, and their wisdom is deprived of its freedom by slander, and they are plundered for their superior intelligence without the opportunity of making a defence? They are not wholly to be pitied. What advantage did the Athenians gain from putting Socrates to death? Famine and plague came upon them as a judgment for their crime. What advantage did the men of Samos gain from

burning Pythagoras? In a moment their land was covered with sand. What advantage did the Jews gain from executing their wise king? It was just after that that their kingdom was abolished.

God justly avenged these three wise men. The Athenians died of hunger; the Samians were overwhelmed by the sea; the Jews, ruined and driven from their land, live in complete dispersion. But Socrates did not die; he lived on in the teaching of Plato. Pythagoras did not die; he lived on in the statue of Hera. Nor did the wise king die; he lived on in the teaching which he had given.[11]

Some who refuse to be persuaded by any amount of evidence criticize this passage on the basis that we cannot know for certain that Bar Serapion was talking about Jesus. They say, "He mentioned Socrates and Pythagoras by name. Why not Jesus?" I believe he was talking about Jesus because no one else fits the description Bar Serapion gives. The man he writes about was (1) Jewish, (2) wise, (3) a teacher and (4) a king. Furthermore, he was (5) executed by His own people (6) a short time before "their kingdom was abolished." As we have already seen, Jerusalem was destroyed by the Romans approximately forty years after Jesus' death. Again, no one else's life in all of history fulfills these six descriptions. Because of this, I believe Bar Serapion's letter is an important document when it comes to proving that Jesus was a real person. I also believe that Bar Serapion's account clearly matches what the Bible says about the life and death of Yeshua, and there should be little doubt regarding who this "wise king" was.

Thallus

The historian Thallus, a Gentile contemporary of Josephus, wrote a history of the world beginning with the fall of Troy and ending in the middle of the first century. Sadly, his work has been lost, except for references made by later writers such as Julius Africanus. Africanus wrote his own history of the world around A.D. 220 and quotes Thallus' reference to the three hours of darkness that the Bible says occurred when Jesus was crucified (see Matthew 27:45; Mark 15:33; Luke 23:44). Africanus, a Gentile believer, writes:

> Thallus, in the third book of his histories, explains away this darkness as an eclipse of the sun—unreasonably, it seems to me. . . . For the Hebrews celebrate the Passover on the 14th day according to the moon, and the passion of our Savior falls on the day before the Passover; but an eclipse of the sun takes place only when the moon comes under the sun. And it cannot happen at any other time but in the interval between the first day of the new moon and the last of the old, that is, at their junction: how then should an eclipse be supposed to happen when the moon is almost diametrically opposite the sun? Let opinion pass however; let it carry the majority with it; and let this portent of the world be deemed an eclipse of the sun, like others a portent only to the eye. Phlegon records that, in the time of Tiberius Caesar, at full moon, there was a full eclipse of the sun from the sixth hour to the ninth—manifestly that one of which we speak.[12]

As you can see, the Greeks and Romans of the first century were not superstitious primitives. They had built the foundation of modern science. They knew about mathematics, astronomy and engineering. They understood that an eclipse of the sun was a natural event. They did not look for a supernatural explanation for every extraordinary event. In fact, in the case of Thallus, it seems that he was trying to do the same thing that many scientists continue to do today: Explain away a supernatural event by saying it had a perfectly natural explanation—one which Julius Africanus disputes. But the important point to note here is that Thallus had written about this eclipse at all—most likely because people still remembered it, talked about it and wondered about it years after it happened.

Thallus wrote his history roughly twenty years after the crucifixion of Jesus—close enough that he very well may have been an eyewitness to the sudden darkness that took place the day of Messiah's death, and certainly close enough that he was able to gather testimony of other eyewitnesses. Plus, if there had been no sudden darkness, he would have been challenged by those who had been alive at the time.

Phlegon

The passage from Julius Africanus above raises the question: Who is this Phlegon he talks about? Phlegon was a secular, Gentile historian born around A.D. 80 who authored two books, *Chronicles* and *Olympiads*. He wrote:

> In the fourth year . . . of Olympiad 202, an eclipse of the sun happened, greater and more excellent than any that had happened before it; at the sixth hour, day turned into dark night, so that the stars were seen in the sky, and an earthquake in Bithynia toppled many buildings of the city of Nicaea.[13]

Matthew 27:54 tells us that a great earthquake occurred during the sudden darkness that took place during Yeshua's crucifixion. It seems obvious, then, that Matthew and Phlegon are talking about the same event—an event that had such an impact on the ancient world that historians such as Thallus felt the necessity of trying to explain it away.

Tacitus and Suetonius

Roman senator and historian Cornelius Tacitus is another ancient writer who mentions Jesus. He was born roughly seventy years after the crucifixion and served as the governor of Asia. Among the surviving portions of his writings are *The Annals* and *The Histories*. One important writing of Tacitus that supports the existence of Jesus is found in his reference to Emperor Nero. I talked earlier about this murderous tyrant and the tortures he inflicted on believers.

During Nero's reign, a huge conflagration destroyed three-fourths of the city, and the finger of suspicion was pointed at the emperor. Some believed Nero wanted to destroy Rome in order to obliterate all records of past Roman heroes and rebuild the city as a tribute to himself. Whether or not the rumor was true, Nero needed a scapegoat, and he found one in those who observed the mysterious new religion of Christianity. He blamed them for starting the fire, stirred up public opinion against them, and tortured and murdered thousands of them.

Tacitus writes:

> [Nero] falsely charged with the guilt, and punished with the most exquisite tortures, the persons commonly called Christians. . . . Christus, the founder of the name, was put to death by Pontius Pilate, procurator of Judea in the reign of Tiberius: but the pernicious superstition, repressed for a time, broke out again, not only through Judea, where the mischief originated, but through the city of Rome also.[14]

A contemporary of Tacitus, Suetonius, also writes about this, saying, "Punishment was inflicted on the Christians, a class of men given to a new and mischievous superstition."[15] Suetonius also says of the Emperor Claudius, "Since the Jews constantly made disturbances at the instigation of Chrestus, he expelled them from Rome."[16]

Lucian

Born around A.D. 120, Lucian was a historian, satirist and play-wright. One of his plays, *The Passing of Peregrinus*, is about a cynic philosopher who became a believer in Jesus, rose to a position of leadership within the Church and then abandoned his faith. Lucian writes that Peregrinus learned "the wondrous lore of the Christians." He also refers to Jesus not by name but as the one "whom they [the early believers] still worship, the man who was crucified in Palestine because he introduced this new cult to the world."

Lucian also says of those followers of the Nazarene, "Their first lawgiver persuaded them that they are all brothers . . . after they have thrown over and denied the gods of Greece and have done reverence to that crucified sophist himself and live according to his laws."[17] If Lucian believed that Jesus was a mythical character, he would have said so. Although he obviously did not have faith in Yeshua as the Messiah or Son of God, he clearly believed that Jesus had been a real historical figure.

Pliny the Younger

Pliny the Younger was governor of the Roman provinces of Pontus and Bithynia from A.D. 111 to 113. The following is an excerpt of his letter to Emperor Trajan that also confirms the existence of Jesus' early followers:

> I have never participated in trials of Christians. I there-fore do not know what offenses it is the practice to punish or investigate. . . .
>
> [I]n the case of those who were denounced to me as Christians, I have . . . interrogated these as to whether [or not] they were Christians; those who confessed I inter-rogated a second and a third time, threatening them with

punishment; those who persisted I ordered executed. . . . There were others possessed of the same folly; but because they were Roman citizens, I signed an order for them to be transferred to Rome.

They asserted, however, that the sum and substance of their fault or error had been that they were accustomed to meet on a fixed day before dawn and sing responsively a hymn to Christ as to a god, and to bind themselves by oath. . . . I discovered nothing else but depraved, excessive superstition.

I therefore postponed the investigation and hastened to consult you. . . . [T]he contagion of this superstition has spread not only to the cities but also to the villages and farms. But it seems possible to check and cure it.[18]

ALBERT EINSTEIN ON JESUS

Let me tell you about one Jew who thought the "Jesus is a myth" theory was nonsense. I am sure you have heard of him.

In an interview with the *Saturday Evening Post*, Albert Einstein was asked if he believed that Jesus had been a historical figure. "Absolutely!" he responded. "No one can read the gospels without feeling the actual presence of Jesus. His personality pulsates in every word. No myth is filled with such life."

In the same interview, Einstein said, "I am a Jew, but I am enthralled by the luminous figure of the Nazarene."[19]

EYEWITNESSES UNTO DEATH

Another important evidence for Jesus' existence can be found in the lives and deaths of those who knew Him best. In 1 Corinthians 15:3–6, Paul declares that he was teaching what had been passed on to him:

For what I received I passed on to you as of first importance: that Christ died for our sins according to the Scriptures,
that he was buried, that he was raised on the third day according to the Scriptures, and that he appeared to Peter, and then
to the Twelve. *After that, he appeared to more than five hundred
of the brothers at the same time, most of whom are still living,
though some have fallen asleep* [emphasis mine].

How could Paul write a passage like this if, in fact, he was pro-
mulgating a myth? If he was not stating the truth, he would have
been successfully challenged by those many eyewitnesses of the risen
Messiah who were still alive when he wrote this passage.

Furthermore, the deaths of those men who spent three years
with Him as members of His closest group of twelve disciples speak
volumes of their faith. Most of these men were martyred for their
faith, often in gruesome ways. Why would these men suffer such
violent deaths in order to perpetuate a myth? It seems obvious that
they would have exposed the myth in order to save their lives. We
do not know for certain how all of these men died, but we do have
strong historical evidence of the following:

1. Peter insisted that he was not worthy to die in the same
   manner in which his Lord had died, and so he was crucified upside down.

2. James, the brother of John, both of whom were sons of
   Zebedee, is believed to be the first of the apostles to die
   (other than Judas, who hanged himself after betraying
   Jesus). Tradition has it that he was beheaded by Herod
   Agrippa I a little more than a decade after Yeshua was
   crucified.

3. James the Less (son of Alphaeus) was thrown from the
   Temple, stoned and beaten with a club.

4. Philip was crucified in Hierapolis, or what is now Turkey.

It is thought that he was 87 years old when he was martyred.

5. Bartholomew was skinned alive and then crucified around A.D. 68.

6. Thomas, who had once said he would not believe until he had seen the resurrected Messiah with his own eyes, was killed with a spear, most likely in India near modern-day Madras.

7. Although he lived to a ripe old age, the apostle John was exiled to the Island of Patmos for his faith. He was willing to endure exile rather than renounce his Messiah. He lived to write the gospel of John, the first, second, and third epistles of John and Revelation, which he wrote to encourage those followers of Yeshua who were struggling with severe persecution for their faith. He is believed to be the last of the original twelve disciples to die, around the year A.D. 100.

8. Finally, the apostle Paul, who was of course not one of the original Twelve but arguably a disciple in his own right and the New Testament writer who had the most significant influence on Christian thinking, was beheaded in Rome by order of the Emperor Nero.[20]

Why would these men willingly suffer so terribly and give their lives simply to preserve a myth? The only answer to their willingness was that they believed with all their hearts that Yeshua was the Messiah who was promised to Israel and that they had been called by God Himself—the God of Abraham, Isaac and Jacob—to proclaim the Good News even unto death.

OVERWHELMING EVIDENCE

The extra-biblical evidence for Yeshua's existence is overwhelming. I hope that the discussion I have outlined in this chapter sufficiently counters any arguments or doubts that Jesus never existed. Understand that this is a controversial topic that pushes people's buttons—especially Jewish people.

Be prepared to encounter anger. Anger seems to be a standard characteristic of those who do not believe in Jesus' existence. If you go online and search "evidence for Jesus' existence," for example, you will find dozens of websites that still insist He never lived. Most of them have one thing in common: anger. They are strident and dismissive of anyone who proclaims true faith and biblical truth.

I have encountered a great deal of anger during my travels for Jewish Voice Ministries, in which I have met quite a few atheists. I honestly cannot recall one atheist who was not mad about something. I have wondered, *If you really think God does not exist, then why are you so mad at Him?* Anger and solid scholarship simply do not go together. It is impossible to reconcile the two. On several occasions I have actually had the joyful privilege of leading some of these atheists to the Lord as the power of God came upon them. I watched them be transformed, literally, in the twinkling of an eye. Human intellect is no match for the power of God's Spirit.

And human intellect cannot disprove the overwhelming evidence to support the existence of Yeshua.

MORE FAITH NOT TO BELIEVE

As I stated before, ultimately belief in Yeshua comes down to a step of faith. If one looks at the evidence with an open mind, however, I believe it takes more faith not to believe than to believe. To reject Yeshua's existence is to close one's eyes to an entire mountain of convincing evidence.

The reality is that the birth and life of this man, Jesus of Nazareth, marks the dividing line of history. The fact that we measure time by His birth is a remarkable example of His reality and importance to the world. It is absolutely astounding to me that this Man from Galilee, who never wrote a book, published an article, or appeared in the media, is without question the most famous individual of all time.

10

BIBLICAL PROPHECY AND THE MESSIAH

For the devout Jews gathered in the Crown Heights section of Brooklyn, New York, it was as if the world had come to an end. They tore their clothing, weeping in agony. "Our Messiah is gone!" they lamented. This was the scene in 1994 as devout followers of Rebbe Menachem Mendel Schneerson (1902–1994) laid their beloved leader to rest. *Rebbe* is a Hebrew word meaning "spiritual leader."

His legacy deeply polarized Orthodox Judaism in America. His devoted followers believed him to be the promised Jewish Messiah, and Chabad Messianists awaited his return from the dead as a Messianic figure. "He will rise again! He is the Messiah!" many proclaimed at his death. But he was not the Messiah, and he was not resurrected.

For centuries, the Jewish people have been looking for Messiah's arrival. Why, then, do most of them reject Jesus of Nazareth? In fact, most Western Jews today, who are for the most part unobservant and secularized, have reduced the expectation of a literal Messiah to nothing more than the hope of a utopian society. The only Jews who are truly seeking a physical or literal Messiah are the ultra-Orthodox, who make up only 10 to 15 percent of the world Jewish population.

The concept of the Messiah in Judaism today, let alone the determination of His identity, is a complex issue. The only thing that is true of most Jews is that they have decided who the Messiah is *not*—and that person is Jesus of Nazareth. I have already explained why this is the case, and it is largely because of the two-thousand-year legacy of hatred in the name of Christ and Christianity.

But who does the Bible say the Messiah will be? What do the Hebrew prophets say about Him? What did the Jewish people expect Him to do? To accomplish? And how did the historical context of Jesus' time affect their expectation? Only by familiarizing ourselves with the Messianic prophecies in Scripture can we firmly establish that Yeshua is the long-awaited Messiah of Israel.

TWO TYPES OF MESSIANIC PROPHECIES

If we rewind to the time of Jesus, we will see some reasons why many Jewish people did not receive Him as their long-awaited Messiah. When Jesus came on the scene, Israel was a subjugated nation that had been conquered by Rome. This meant that they lived without the rights of self-rule and freedom of religious practice. It is likely that the predominant view in that day was that the Messiah would be a mighty king who would conquer Rome and usher in an era of peace. This Redeemer would restore the Davidic kingdom. Like King David before Him, He would usher in Israel's return to its former prominence.

Instead, Jesus came as a humble rabbi—a suffering Servant—who was destined to give His life as the Lamb of God to take away the sins of Israel and the world. What can be confusing is the fact that Scripture depicts the coming Messiah in two ways—as *both* suffering Servant and conquering King. And the Bible offers no chronological order to process this division.

That said, it is not difficult to divide these Messianic prophecies into two distinct columns. Scholars refer to the first set of passages as the prophecies of Messiah ben-Joseph, the son of Joseph. The reason for this title is that His life parallels that of the Old Testament hero, Joseph. You may remember that Joseph was rejected by his brothers and falsely imprisoned, but then ultimately rose to glory.

The other passages that portray a Messiah of influence, power, righteousness and deliverance are called the prophecies of Messiah ben-David. This group incorporates the Messianic prophecies that parallel the life of King David. Under David's rule, Israel reached its apex—its Golden Age. In the first century, under Rome's oppressive thumb, the Jews were looking for this Messiah ben-David to come in power and restore Israel to its rightful place as the head among the nations.

In rabbinic literature predating the time of Jesus, the rabbis dealt with these seemingly conflicting Messianic prophecies in this way: Two Messiahs would come, Messiah ben-Joseph, who would suffer and die, followed by Messiah ben-David, who would come in power, glory and justice. Messiah ben-Joseph (who had died) would be resurrected, and the two would rule together over Israel.

Keep in mind that these are all *ancient* views that were held *before* the time of Jesus. They are no longer considered valid by anyone in the Jewish community. Most have abandoned altogether the idea of a redeeming Messiah.

But the ancient rabbis were not that far from the truth. They concluded there would be two Messiahs. We know now there will be one Messiah, but He will come twice. He came first as Messiah ben-Joseph, the Lamb of God who would take away the sins of the world. One day soon He will return as Messiah ben-David, the conquering Messiah, who will defeat the enemies of God and establish His millennial Kingdom on this earth for a thousand years.

ISAIAH'S SUFFERING SERVANT SONGS

The ancient rabbis understood the valid Messianic prophecies that portrayed a suffering Messiah. In the Babylonian Talmud the question is asked, "Where do I find the Messiah?" The reply cites Isaiah 53: "He is sitting among the poor lepers" (Sanhedrin 98a).

Let's take a closer look at some of the Old Testament prophecies regarding Messiah—starting with those that present Him as a humble Servant reaching out to a lost world. Several of the most important prophetic passages are the four "Servant Songs" found in the book of Isaiah. These songs contain a mixture throughout of both Messianic identities, Messiah ben-Joseph and Messiah ben-David.

THE FIRST SERVANT SONG

The first of these songs is Isaiah 42:1–7:

> Here is my servant, whom I uphold,
>   my chosen one in whom I delight;
> I will put my Spirit on him
>   and he will bring justice to the nations.
>
> He will not shout or cry out,
>   or raise his voice in the streets.

A bruised reed he will not break,
and a smoldering wick he will not snuff out.
In faithfulness he will bring forth justice;

He will not falter or be discouraged
till he establishes justice on earth.
In his law the islands will put their hope.

This is what God the LORD says—
he who created the heavens and stretched them out,
who spread out the earth and all that comes out of it,
who gives breath to its people,
and life to those who walk on it:

"I, the LORD, have called you in righteousness;
I will take hold of your hand.
I will keep you and will make you
to be a covenant for the people
and a light for the Gentiles,

to open eyes that are blind,
to free captives from prison
and to release from the dungeon those
who sit in darkness."

These seven verses give a clear picture of the life of Jesus as told within the pages of the New Testament—the meek rabbi from Nazareth who went around doing good, healing, delivering those who were oppressed and teaching the Kingdom of God. He brought hope and freedom to those trapped in spiritual darkness—the sinners of His time—prostitutes, tax collectors and, occasionally, a Gentile, although His earthly mission was to the lost sheep of the house of Israel.

THE SECOND SERVANT SONG

The next Servant Song is found in Isaiah 49, where the Servant himself speaks about how God has called Him to bring salvation, not only to the people of Israel, but to the Gentiles as well. In the first verse of the chapter, He says, "Listen to me, you islands; hear this, you distant nations: Before I was born the LORD called me; from my birth He has made mention of my name."

I am especially fond of the final two verses of this passage, in which the Messiah speaks of His mission:

> And now the LORD says—
> he who formed me in the womb to be his servant
> to bring Jacob back to him
> and gather Israel to himself,
> for I am honored in the eyes of the LORD
> and my God has been my strength—he says:
> "It is too small a thing for you to be my servant
> to restore the tribes of Jacob
> and bring back those of Israel I have kept.
> I will also make you a light for the Gentiles,
> that you may bring my salvation to the ends of the earth."
> —ISAIAH 49:5–6

My Jewish friends have occasionally told me, "Jesus may be the Messiah for the Gentiles, and that is fine, but He is not our Messiah." And yet, right here in this passage the great Jewish prophet Isaiah clearly says that the Messiah will bring *both* Israel and the Gentiles back into a right relationship with God. This is reiterated in the New Testament by Yeshua Himself, who said, "I am the way and the truth and the life. *No one comes to the Father except through me*" (John 14:6, emphasis mine).

Also, the apostle Paul writes in Romans 1:16, "I am not ashamed of the gospel, because it is the power of God for the salvation of everyone who believes: *first for the Jew,* then for the Gentile" (emphasis mine).

Remember that God used the Jewish people to bring the Messiah into the world and the Jewish disciples to take the Gospel to the remote corners of the earth. It is fair to say to the Gentile believer who is reading this that you believe in the God of Israel today because the first Jewish followers of Yeshua brought the Gospel to your ancestors.

Paul makes it clear in Romans 11:11 that it is through the "transgression" of Israel that "salvation has come to the Gentiles," with a responsibility to provoke the Jewish people to jealousy. What does Paul mean? He means simply that believing Gentiles should live a life that mirrors the love, compassion, power, sense of purpose and destiny that Yeshua Himself portrayed. This will draw Jewish people to Him.

God calls us Jews the Chosen People. That term always intrigued me. When I was a child, I asked my teacher in synagogue what it meant. "We are chosen to be persecuted," she replied.

I thought, *If that is what I was chosen for, then I do not want to be a Jew anymore.* My teacher did not understand that God chose us to be a light to the nations of the world—to reveal the one true God of creation, the God of Abraham, Isaac and Jacob, and to bring the nations to Him.

As a Jew, I am still in awe when I read words like these from Bernard B. Gair, a Jewish believer in Messiah who once served as president of the Hebrew Christian Alliance of America:

> In His infinite wisdom God chose from among all the peoples of the earth a people insignificant from the standpoint of political, economic, cultural and military power. He chose Israel to be the instrument of human redemption. . . . Israel would prepare the way for the coming of a Deliverer, or Messiah. . . . The Messiah would provide atonement, reconciliation and restoration.[1]

... How could the people of Israel recognize the Redeemer when He came? God revealed in the Old Testament in utmost detail how, where, and under what circumstances Messiah would come.[2]

THE THIRD SERVANT SONG

The third of the four Servant Songs is found in Isaiah 50:4–9. Here, Messiah (clearly falling under the Messiah ben-Joseph heading) says that He will not be deterred from finishing the task that has been set before Him. In verses six through nine, He says:

> I offered my back to those who beat me,
> my cheeks to those who pulled out my beard;
> I did not hide my face
> from mocking and spitting.
>
> Because the Sovereign LORD helps me
> I will not be disgraced.
> Therefore have I set my face like flint,
> and I know I will not be put to shame.
>
> He who vindicates me is near.
> Who then will bring charges against me?
> Let us face each other!
> Who is my accuser?
> Let him confront me!
>
> It is the Sovereign LORD who helps me
> Who is he that will condemn me?
> They will all wear out like a garment;
> the moths will eat them up.

I will never forget the chill that ran down my spine the first time I read these words and realized that Isaiah was writing about what Yeshua had endured for me as a sinner! Every time I read this passage and the words that follow them through Isaiah 52 and 53, I sit in awe of the great sacrifice that Yeshua made for us.

THE FOURTH SERVANT SONG

As we move into chapter 52, we read, "See, my servant will act wisely; he will be raised and lifted up and highly exalted" (Isaiah 52:13). We see here in the first verse of the "Suffering Servant" passage that, like Joseph, the Messiah will ultimately be exalted not only by the Gentiles, but also by Israel. The Bible clearly outlines this in other verses such as Zechariah 12, which says that [Israel] will "look on me, the one they have pierced, and they will mourn for him as one mourns for an only child." Jeremiah 31:34 tells us that everyone will know Him, "from the least of them to the greatest." And in Romans 11:26, Paul says, "All Israel will be saved."

Isaiah 52 then shifts to His rejection: "There were many who were appalled at him—his appearance was so disfigured beyond that of any man and his form marred beyond human likeness" (v. 14). This is a picture of the Messiah on the cross, following His judgment, beating, ridicule and the plucking out of His beard. He endured greater physical torment than any of us can imagine.

The poem continues:

> So will he sprinkle many nations,
>   and kings will shut their mouths because of him.
>   For what they were not told, they will see,
>   and what they have not heard, they will understand.
>
> Who has believed our message
>   and to whom has the arm of the LORD been revealed?
>
> He grew up before him like a tender shoot,
>   and like a root out of dry ground.
>   He had no beauty or majesty to attract us to him,
>   nothing in his appearance that we should desire him.

> He was despised and rejected by men,
>> a man of sorrows, and familiar with suffering.
>> Like one from whom men hide their faces
>> he was despised, and we esteemed him not.
>
> —Isaiah 52:15–53:3

This is a powerful prophecy of Israel's rejection of Yeshua as its Messiah, written more than seven hundred years before He was born. Although many did follow Him, the vast majority of Israel was led away from Him by the Sadducees and the Pharisees. Clearly, He is the most embraced and rejected figure of all human history.

The text goes on to prophesy:

> Surely he took up our infirmities
>> and carried our sorrows,
>> yet we considered him stricken by God,
>> smitten by him, and afflicted.
>
> But he was pierced for our transgressions,
>> he was crushed for our iniquities;
>> the punishment that brought us peace was upon him,
>> and by his wounds we are healed.
>
> —Isaiah 53:4–5

This is an accurate picture of Yeshua's crucifixion and substitutionary atonement for us. We are told in 2 Corinthians 5:21 that He who knew no sin became sin that we might be made the righteousness of God in Him (paraphrased). God laid upon Him our iniquity, but the people of His day thought He was being punished for His own acts of rebellion against Roman rule and authority, as well as against Jewish religious authority. This passage is paralleled in Daniel 9:26.

This passage of Isaiah perfectly parallels the descriptions of the gospels, which are detailed in relating that Jesus' hands and feet were pierced by the Romans in preparation for His crucifixion (also see Psalm 22:16). The "crushing" mentioned in Isaiah 53:5 could refer to the effects of suffocation from being hanged in such a fashion.

Allow me to revert to something else at this point. In chapter 4 I mentioned that the eleventh-century rabbi Rashi's interpretation of Isaiah 53 said that he believed the passage meant the Messiah was supposed to come but had not. Rashi later redefined the suffering Servant as the nation of Israel, but until that time (the eleventh century), most everyone agreed that this passage in Isaiah was talking about Messiah. In fact, Rashi met with great resistance to this interpretation at first, but eventually it was adopted as the accepted interpretation within Judaism. This was in great part due to an effort to distance the Jewish community from the Christian interpretation.

The text says He was pierced, crushed and punished for *our* transgressions, and that His wounds brought healing to us! Who is "He" and "we"? This has to be a Redeemer who is paying the price for the iniquities of Israel. He, the Messiah, was pierced for our [Israel's] iniquities. We [Israel] considered Him stricken, smitten and afflicted, but He [The Messiah] was pierced for our [Israel's] transgressions. He was crushed for the iniquities of the nation of Israel, and the punishment that brought us [Israel] peace was upon Him, the Messiah, and by His [the Messiah's] wounds, we [Israel] are healed.

Isaiah 53 continues with verse 6:

> We all, like sheep, have gone astray,
>   each of us has turned to his own way;
> and the LORD has laid on him
>   the iniquity of us all.

Considered in context, this passage is referring to the sin of Israel, and yet it also has a broader application, since all of us have sinned and come short of the glory of God. This is a spiritual reality as true as gravity. It was certainly in the heart of God that His atonement would be for all mankind because "God so loved the world that he gave his one and only Son, that whoever believes in him shall not perish but have eternal life" (John 3:16).

The next passage puts an end once and for all to the myth that the Jews killed Jesus:

> He was oppressed and afflicted,
>> yet he did not open his mouth;
>> he was led like a lamb to the slaughter,
>> and as a sheep before her shearers is silent,
>> so he did not open his mouth.
>
> —Isaiah 53:7

We see from this that no one man or people are responsible for the death of Jesus. He chose to lay down His life for us, to eternally pay the price for you and me.

The accuracy and the detail of Isaiah 53 are astounding to me. And the gospels go to equally detailed lengths to show that Isaiah 53 is fulfilled. Isaiah specifically mentions in verse 9, for example, that the Messiah would be assigned a grave with the wicked (the two thieves crucified on either side of Him) and the rich (buried in the tomb owned by Joseph of Arimathea), "though he had done no violence, nor was any deceit in his mouth." For God to give us these signs in such detail indicates that He wants to reveal His Messiah to those who are willing to look for Him with an open heart and mind.

Some rabbis have looked at these Servant passages in Isaiah and suggested that the prophet had a particular king in mind—perhaps Hezekiah, Uzziah, Jehoiachin, Zerubbabel or Cyrus. I am frankly amazed that so many Jewish scholars have rejected what seems to me the obvious interpretation. Because they cannot accept that Isaiah was looking ahead to the life of Yeshua, they come up with all sorts of theories that simply do not fit the description.

I believe there is only one person in all of history whose life is reflected in Isaiah's words, and that is Jesus of Nazareth.

OTHER FULFILLED PROPHECIES

The suffering Servant passages in Isaiah are just a few of the many Old Testament Scriptures that Jesus fulfilled. In fact, the Bible contains more than three hundred of them—and Yeshua fulfilled every one of them that related to His first coming. And when He returns, He will fulfill the rest.

First, the Old Testament was clear that the Messiah would be born in Bethlehem: "But you, Bethlehem Ephrathah, though you are small among the clans of Judah, out of you will come for me one who will be ruler over Israel, whose origins are from of old, from ancient times" (Micah 5:2). As you know, Jesus was born in Bethlehem, in the line of David.

Furthermore, scholars of that time expected that Messiah would be born in Bethlehem. When Herod summoned the wise men of Israel to find out where his competitor would come from, they immediately responded, "Bethlehem." Why? They knew Micah's prophecy.

Some of my Jewish friends argue that this verse is talking about King David. This cannot be the case, however, because this passage in Micah is a predictive prophecy that points to the future, and it was written several centuries *after* David had died.

Something else to notice about this prophecy is the peculiar statement that although He would come out of Bethlehem, His goings forth would be from old, from everlasting (in Hebrew, *olam*). In other words, even though He would be born in Bethlehem, He had a preexistent nature. We see the same thing in Isaiah 9:6, where we read that unto us a Son would be born, a child would be given, but He would be the everlasting God.

The rabbis have struggled a great deal with this passage. Some have argued that nothing in Jewish literature speaks of Messiah being divine or God Himself, and while there is a ring of truth to this, there seemed to be an understanding among the ancient rabbis that the Messiah would be preexistent based on these texts.

Among the other prophecies He fulfilled, Yeshua:

- **was rejected** by His own (see Isaiah 53:3)

- **is the Stone** the builders rejected, which then became the Capstone (see Psalm 118:22–23)

- **is the gentle King** who entered Jerusalem riding on a donkey (see Zechariah 9:9)

- **was betrayed** by a friend (see Psalm 41:9)

- **was betrayed** for thirty pieces of silver (see Zechariah 11:12–13)

- **was accused** by false witnesses (see Psalm 35:11)

- **was hated** without a cause (see Psalm 35:19)

- **was pierced** (see Zechariah 12:10; Psalm 22:16)

- **felt thirsty** during His execution (see Psalm 22:15)

- **looked on** as soldiers gambled for His garment (see Psalm 22:18)

- **cried,** "My God, my God, why have You forsaken Me?" (Psalm 22:1)

I have only scratched the surface. Every Messianic prophecy relating to the suffering Servant was fulfilled in great detail by Jesus of Nazareth during His time on earth.

THE PROPHECIES YESHUA DID NOT FULFILL

As I mentioned at the beginning of this chapter, other Messianic prophecies have not yet come to pass. Jewish leaders often cite these prophecies to support their contention that Jesus is not the Messiah. Those of us who embrace Yeshua and believe in the writings of the Brit Chadashah (the New Testament) as well as the Tanakh (Old Testament) understand that such prophecies will be fulfilled when He returns to earth a second time—and that His return is near. But until He does, some prophecies will remain "unfulfilled." Let's take a look at a few of these.

He Would Establish an Earthly Kingdom

During Jesus' earthly ministry, many of His Jewish followers thought He would ultimately deliver them from the hands of Rome. When they saw that this was not the case, many deserted and turned against Him. Even His own disciples did not understand that He would suffer and die. They thought He would fulfill the role of Messiah ben-David. That is why they argued over which of them would be greatest in the Kingdom (see Luke 9:46–48) and why the last thing they asked Yeshua before His ascension was, "Lord, are you at this time going to restore the kingdom to Israel?" (see Acts 1:6). As believers, we know that Jesus will indeed establish His earthly Kingdom when He returns in the last days.

He Would Gather the Dispersed Jews (see Isaiah 43:5–6)

In the Old Testament, the Jews were dispersed to remote parts of the earth, first through the Assyrian invasion of Israel and then when Babylon conquered Judah. A remnant eventually returned, but later, when the Roman army destroyed the Temple and much of Jerusalem in A.D. 70, thousands of Jews were killed, and many of the survivors were sent into exile as slaves. They were scattered throughout the Roman Empire and the world. Eventually only a few thousand Jews were left in their own land.

The Hebrew Scriptures foretell this dispersion. Hosea 3:4–5, for example, predicts:

> The Israelites will live many days without king or prince, without sacrifice. . . . Afterward [they] will return and seek the LORD their God. . . . They will come trembling to the LORD and to his blessings in the last days.

This and many other Scriptures like it are being fulfilled today.

Those who had been scattered never forgot about Israel and prayed daily that they would one day be able to return to their beloved land. Their prayers were answered in stages: first, in 1917, when the Balfour Declaration called for the establishment of a Jewish homeland in Israel; and second, when the State of Israel was established supernaturally in 1948 (see Isaiah 66:8). Today almost six million Jews live in Israel, and they have come from all over the world. Dozens of prophecies throughout the Hebrew Scriptures promise the return of the Jewish people to their homeland in the last days, and we are now seeing these prophecies fulfilled before our very eyes.

Jeremiah 16:14–15 is another of these prophecies:

> Days are coming . . . when men will no longer say, "As surely as the LORD lives, who brought the Israelites up out of Egypt," but they will say, "As surely as the LORD lives, who brought the Israelites up out of the land of the north and out of all the countries where he had banished them."

It is no coincidence that a vertical line drawn on a map from Israel due north intersects Moscow in Russia. The largest *aliyah* (return to Israel) in the history of the modern state of Israel is from the northern land of Russia. Indeed, more than one million Russian-speaking Jews have come home to Israel from the republics of the former Soviet Union—so many, in fact, that they have changed the face of the nation of Israel. Many road signs in Israel are now translated into Russian, in addition to Hebrew and Arabic. The last time I passed through customs at the Tel Aviv airport, I stood in a line for Israeli citizens and heard no Hebrew—only Russian. God is fulfilling His promise of Jeremiah 16:15 in restoring His people from the land of the north.

Isaiah 11:11 is another work in progress. It says,

> The LORD will reach out his hand a second time to
> reclaim the remnant that is left of his people from Assyria,
> from Lower Egypt, from Upper Egypt, from Cush, from
> Elam, from Babylonia, from Hamath and from the islands of
> the sea.

The so-called "lost tribes" of Israel are being uncovered in the most remote places in the world. More than 130,000 *Beta Israel* Jews from Ethiopia, for example, have returned to Israel over the last twenty years. Another example is the *Bnei Menashe* in Manipur and Mizoram, India. This large community, which may number as many as one to two million, claims to be descended from the "lost tribe" of Manasseh (Joseph's oldest son and Jacob's grandson) and has allowed several thousand to emigrate to Israel. Indeed, prophecy is being fulfilled before our very eyes.

He Would Bring World Peace (see Isaiah 2:1–4)

The most common argument I hear against Jesus being the Messiah is that He did not bring peace to the world. Isaiah 2:1–4 and Micah 4:3 talk about a time when swords will be beaten into plowshares and spears into pruning hooks. This same utopian society of world peace is described in Isaiah 11:6–9:

> The wolf will live with the lamb, the leopard will lie down with the goat, the calf and the lion and the yearling together; and a little child will lead them. The cow will feed with the bear, their young will lie down together, and the lion will eat straw like the ox. The infant will play near the hole of the cobra, and the young child put his hand into the viper's nest. They will neither harm nor destroy on all my holy mountain, for the earth will be full of the knowledge of the LORD as the waters cover the sea.

Looking at the current condition of the earth, no one can argue the fact that these prophecies have not yet been fulfilled. But I am convinced that fulfillment is near.

In Revelation 19:11–15, the apostle John gives us a glorious picture of what it will be like when Yeshua returns to fulfill these prophecies:

> I saw heaven standing open and there before me was a white horse, whose rider is called Faithful and True. With justice he judges and makes war. His eyes are like blazing fire, and on his head are many crowns. He has a name written on him that no one knows but he himself. He is dressed in a robe dipped in blood, and his name is the Word of God. The armies of heaven were following him, riding on white horses and dressed in fine linen, white and clean. Out of his mouth comes a sharp sword with which to strike down the nations. "He will rule them with an iron scepter." He treads the winepress of the fury of the wrath of God Almighty.

Many other biblical passages prophesy Messiah's return. They are frightening in many ways because they relate to the raging fire of God's wrath and the destruction of His enemies. Jeremiah says,

"How awful that day will be! None will be like it. It will be a time of trouble for Jacob, but he will be saved out of it" (Jeremiah 30:7).

IF JESUS IS NOT MESSIAH, THEN WHO IS?

In chapter 4 we talked about an important prophecy from the book of Daniel that set a time frame for Messiah's arrival. In his book *Answering Jewish Objections to Jesus*, Michael Brown gives even more solid evidence that Jewish scholars expected Messiah's arrival during the time of the Second Temple.[3] He begins by looking at a prophecy from Haggai 2:

> "In a little while I will once more shake the heavens and the earth, the sea and the dry land. I will shake all nations, and the desired of all nations will come, and I will fill this house with glory," says the Lord Almighty. . . . "The glory of this present house will be greater than the glory of the former house."
>
> —Haggai 2:6–9

The "house" to which Haggai refers is the Second Temple, which was destroyed by the Romans in A.D. 70. The "desired of all nations" refers to the Messiah.

Brown points out that rabbis have spent much time wrestling with this verse, trying to figure out how this Second Temple could have surpassed the glory of the Temple built by Solomon, which was destroyed by the Babylonians. As Brown points out, Solomon's Temple contained a number of important holy objects that were missing from the Second Temple, including the Ark of the Covenant, the Urim and Thummim and the Mercy Seat.

Furthermore, the Shekinah glory of God was present in Solomon's Temple. Second Chronicles 7:1–3 tells us what happened on the day the Temple was dedicated:

> When Solomon finished praying, fire came down from
> heaven and consumed the burnt offering and the sacrifices,
> and the glory of the Lord filled the temple. . . . When all the
> Israelites saw the fire coming down and the glory of the Lord
> above the temple, they knelt on the pavement with their faces
> to the ground, and they worshiped.

Nothing of the sort happened at the dedication of the second
Temple, so how could its glory have surpassed that of the first Temple? To find the answer, Brown turns to Malachi 3:1–4:

> "I will send my messenger, who will prepare the way
> before me. Then suddenly the Lord you are seeking will come
> to his temple; the messenger of the covenant, whom you desire,
> will come," says the Lord Almighty. But who can endure the
> day of his coming? . . . For he will be like a refiner's fire or a
> launderer's soap. He will sit as a refiner and purifier of sil-
> ver. . . . Then the Lord will have men who will bring offerings
> in righteousness, and the offerings of Judah and Jerusalem will
> be acceptable to the Lord . . . as in former years.

Brown says that "according to the famous medieval Jewish com-
mentaries of Radak (David Kimchi) and Metsudat David," the words
"the Lord" in the second sentence of this passage refer to the Messiah.
Brown writes, "The glory of the Second Temple would be greater
than the glory of the First Temple because the Lord Himself—in
the person of the Messiah—would visit the Second Temple."[4] Of
course, this had to happen prior to A.D. 70, because that was the year
the Second Temple ceased to exist!

If we accept these passages as accurate, then either Jesus is the
Messiah, or the title belongs to someone else who lived on earth
when He did. And who else could it possibly be? Others have claimed
to be the Messiah, but not one comes within light years of fulfilling
the qualifications the way Jesus of Nazareth does.

THREE FALSE MESSIAHS

Several men have either claimed to be Messiah or have been looked to by many Jews as Messiah. One of these men was Simon bar Kochba, who led a revolt against Rome in the second century. As one would expect, his revolt was short-lived and came to a brutal end. According to Jewish historians, many people were burned alive, wrapped in Torah scrolls. Cassius Dio, writing a century later, reported that more than 580,000 people were killed. It is impossible to know if that number is accurate, although archeologists have found mass graves at several locations throughout the city.[5]

Another who claimed to be Messiah was Shabbethai Zebi. He lived about 1,600 years too late, but at the height of his popularity thousands followed him. He openly proclaimed himself as Messiah and wrote a letter that said:

> The first-begotten Son of God, Shabbethai Zebi, Messiah and Redeemer of the people of Israel, to all the sons of Israel, Peace! Since ye have been deemed worthy to behold the great day and the fulfilment of God's word by the Prophets, your lament and sorrow must be changed into joy, and your fasting into merriment; for ye shall weep no more. Rejoice with song and melody, and change the day formerly spent in sadness and sorrow into a day of jubilee, because I have appeared.[6]

His followers were disillusioned when this would-be Messiah was ordered to convert to Islam or face imprisonment or death. He chose to convert and then wrote to his followers, "God has made me an Ishmaelite; He commanded, and it was done."[7] For a while he tried to walk a tightrope between both faiths. He told the Muslims that he was maintaining contact with Jews only because he wanted to convert them, and told the Jews he was only pretending to be a Muslim so that he might bring them to Judaism. It was not long before both groups grew tired of him and he vanished into history.[8]

Finally, the most recent of the false rabbis was the late Rabbi Menachem Schneerson, whom I mentioned at the beginning of this chapter. While the rabbi himself did not claim to be Messiah, many of his followers clearly thought this was the case—and some still do. After he died in 1994 they expected that he would rise from the dead. Many of them are still waiting.

JESUS IS THE ONLY LOGICAL MESSIAH

The logical conclusion to be drawn from all of this is that only one Person perfectly fits the prophets' description of the Messiah—and that is Jesus of Nazareth.

What joy there will be when those of us who know Him now as the Lamb of God who has taken away our sins welcome His return as the Lion of Judah! God forbid that anyone should wait and have to face the Lion of Judah without having first known Him as the Lamb.

WHATEVER HAPPENED TO JUDAISM?

Many Jews—and non-Jews too—believe that the Judaism being practiced today is the same religion that was observed by Moses, David, Solomon and all the other great heroes of the Bible. It is not. Though there are many common threads, there are also some important and fundamental differences.

THE ORIGINS OF RABBINIC JUDAISM

The Judaism now practiced by most Jews in the world today is rabbinic Judaism. In other words, modern Jews have placed the oral traditions of the rabbis on the same level with the teachings in the Torah. In fact, such teachings actually are given more weight than the teachings of Torah. Rabbinic Judaism has replaced the scriptural requirement for blood atonement with *teshuva* (repentance), *tefillah* (prayer) and *mitzvot* (good deeds). The result is that the entire sacrificial system God established has been replaced by an artificial, man-made one. And subsequently, if there is no need for blood sacrifice, then there is no need for a Savior. Indeed, many contemporary Jews reject Jesus because their rabbis have taught them that they do not need a Savior.

How did this happen?

That question has no simple answer. But looking at the origins of rabbinic Judaism is helpful.

If one man should be singled out as the founder of rabbinic Judaism, it would be Rabbi Yochanan ben Zakkai. The first leader of the rabbinical academy at Yabneh, which was established soon after the destruction of the Second Temple, ben Zakkai presided over a council that was instrumental in establishing the first accepted canon of Hebrew Scriptures and laid the foundation for rabbinic Judaism.

Ben Zakkai was born about the time Yeshua was teaching in Jerusalem. A follower of the famous Rabbi Hillel the Elder—who had been Israel's foremost spiritual leader during the years when Jesus was growing up in Nazareth—ben Zakkai was a fiery Pharisee. He passionately opposed the Sadducees and anyone else who disagreed with his views. He lived for a time in Galilee, for example, and denounced the people there for their lack of religious zeal. He said that their secular nature would cause them to fall victim to robbers.

Matthew 15 says that Jesus offended the Pharisees when He said, "Their teachings are but rules taught by men" (Matthew 15:9). He was speaking of the oral law, teachings and traditions that were outside the realm of Scripture and therefore not given by God.

The rabbis believed that two sets of laws, equally important, had been given to Moses at Mount Sinai. The first was the Torah, the initial five books of the *Tanakh,* which were written by Moses. The second was the oral law, which, according to their tradition, was given to Moses with the Torah at Mount Sinai. A simple way to understand the oral law, called the *Mishna* and later codified into a volume of writings called the Talmud (made up of the *Mishna* and the *Gemara*), is to see it as a rabbinic commentary on the Torah, or rabbinic arguments regarding how the Scriptures should be appropriately applied.

According to the rabbis, the Torah has 613 commandments, 248 that are positive and 365 that are negative. The rabbis were so concerned about the most minute violation of these commandments that they created what many have called "a fence around the law." But this oral law became so far removed from the original intent of the Scriptures that it led to a religion that was ruled by the letter of the law, rather than the spirit of the law.

Despite Ben Zakkai's passionate personality, he was not interested in fighting the Romans, most likely because he understood the overwhelming odds the Jews were facing. When invading troops laid siege to Jerusalem prior to the Temple's destruction, Ben Zakkai spoke openly in favor of peace. This enraged many in Jerusalem—so many, in fact, that he feared for his safety. He arranged for his followers to announce that he had died and then to carry him out of the city in a coffin. Once outside the city gates, the rabbi emerged from his hiding place and made his way to the tent of Vespasian, commander of the Roman forces.

He told Vespasian that God had revealed that the commander would soon become the new emperor of Rome. Then, having ingratiated himself in this way, he asked for a favor. He told the Roman general that he knew the fate about to befall Israel and asked him to spare the city of Yabneh, along with a group of leading rabbis. This would allow them to establish a school where they could study the Torah in peace.

Vespasian agreed. And when he became emperor upon the death of Vitellius, he kept his word. Yabneh and the rabbis were spared. Ben Zakkai founded his school, and Yabneh became the new center of Judaism.

REPLACING THE SYSTEM OF BLOOD SACRIFICE

After Jerusalem was destroyed, Ben Zakkai and the other rabbis at Yabneh were confronted by some serious issues. How could they breathe new life into the devastated Jewish nation? The war with Rome had left many of their cities and towns in ruins, including their beloved Jerusalem. An estimated 500,000 people had lost their lives.

Council members were also alarmed by the rapid growth of what was later to become Christianity. Many Jews were embracing Yeshua as their promised Messiah, especially in light of His prophecy that the Temple would be destroyed. The rabbis were determined to stop the spread of this new "cult." One way the council tried to do this was by banning the Septuagint, the Greek translation of the Tanakh, which was being used by most of the followers of Messiah—a rather strange step, considering that most Jews could read Greek, but not Hebrew.

Zakkai and the rabbis at Yabneh soon convened to discuss the future of a Judaism that no longer had a Temple, priesthood or sacrificial system. The council was faced with the challenge of preserving Judaism without these essential elements of Jewish life. Ben Zakkai understood that this sacrificial system needed to be replaced in order to preserve the Jewish people. In his effort to bring about this transition, he focused on Hosea 6:6 as an indication that God no longer required such sacrifices: "For I desire mercy, not sacrifice, and acknowledgment of God rather than burnt offerings." Zakkai and the other rabbis reasoned that since God had allowed the Temple to be destroyed, He no longer desired burnt offerings from His people.

Of course, Jews who acknowledged Yeshua as Messiah believed that the Temple sacrifices were no longer necessary because the ultimate sacrifice had already been made. The Lamb of God had shed His blood to forgive their sins. Nothing further was required.

The problem with rabbinic theology in regard to sin and atonement is that it directly contradicts the Torah. Leviticus 17:11 makes this absolutely clear when it states that "the life of a creature is in the blood, and I have given it to you to make atonement for yourselves on the altar; it is the blood that makes atonement for one's life." In fact, all of the covenants that God made with mankind in general, and with Israel specifically, were cut with blood. The very word "covenant," *brit* (בריח) in Hebrew, means "to cut."

In the Adamic Covenant, the first animal had to be sacrificed in order to cover Adam and Eve in their nakedness. The Abrahamic Covenant also was sealed with blood sacrifice. Genesis 15 records that God commanded Abraham to sacrifice a heifer, a goat, a ram, a dove and a pigeon. Abraham slaughtered the animals and waited for God to respond.

> So the Lord said to him, "Bring me a heifer, a goat and a ram, each three years old, along with a dove and a young pigeon." Abram brought all these to him, cut them in two and arranged the halves opposite each other; the birds, however, he did not cut in half. . . . When the sun had set and darkness had fallen, a smoking firepot with a blazing torch appeared and passed between the pieces. On that day the Lord made a covenant with Abram and said, "To your descendants I give this land, from the river of Egypt to the great river, the Euphrates— the land of the Kenites, Kennizzites, Kadmonites, Hittites, Perizzites, Rephaites, Amorites, Canaanites, Girgashites and Jebusites."
>
> —Genesis 15:9–10, 17–21

The Mosaic Covenant also was sealed with the shedding of blood:

> Moses took half of the blood and put it in bowls, and the other half he sprinkled on the altar. Then he took the Book of the Covenant and read it to the people. They responded, "We will do everything the LORD has said; we will obey." Moses then took the blood, sprinkled it on the people and said, "This is the blood of the covenant that the Lord has made with you in accordance with all these words."
>
> —EXODUS 24:6–8

In chapter 4 we discussed the origins of the Passover. The Israelites were spared because they had sprinkled the blood of a lamb on their doorposts. The angel saw the blood, passed over their homes and spared their firstborn sons.

On the Day of Atonement, the high priest would sacrifice a bull and a goat to atone for his sins and the sins of the people. This was an essential part of Jewish life and worship.

The New Covenant, too, is enacted by blood. When Yeshua raised the third cup at Passover (historically, the third cup is for redemption) and declared that this cup now represented His blood, which was shed for them for the forgiveness of sins, He was making a covenant with them. He sealed that covenant the following day when nails were driven through His hands and feet on the cross at Calvary and when the spear was later thrust into His side and blood and water came gushing out.

I cannot emphasize it enough: Blood sacrifice is essential for atonement of sin.

To support their position, the rabbis point to Scriptures such as "I delight in mercy more than offerings." But such Scriptures are not contradicting the need for blood sacrifice. If they are taken in context, it is obvious that the Israelites already assumed blood sacrifice was necessary. The Lord was simply pointing out the importance of right motives and behavior.

These verses were never meant to contradict the need for blood sacrifice. This was, and is to this day, a universal law of God: Without the shedding of blood, there is no forgiveness of sin. And rabbinic Judaism's view of how one atones for sin stands in direct conflict with this biblical standard.

RABBINIC JUDAISM WINS THE DAY

Most historians will tell you that the belief in two laws—one written, the other oral—had been around for centuries prior to the council at Yabneh. While this is somewhat true, the council played a pivotal role in elevating the oral law and turning rabbinic Judaism into the prevailing religion of Israel.

This is still the Judaism that reigns today. Of the estimated 13.3 million Jews in the world, only a handful of those who are observant practice some form other than rabbinic Judaism. One group, called the Karaites, accept only the written Torah as their guide in matters of faith and practice. Although the Karaites were once a significant force in worldwide Judaism, only an estimated 30,000 of them survive today.[1] Clearly, rabbinic Judaism has won out in the battle for the allegiance of the Jewish people, and for centuries this has meant two things: (1) Christians and Jews are distinct and different religions and have little or nothing in common, and (2) Jewish people do not accept Jesus as Israel's Messiah.

According to Louis Goldberg, former professor of theology and Jewish Studies at Moody Bible Institute, part of the intent of rabbinic Judaism "was to discredit the Jewish believers in Jesus the Messiah, particularly, and a belief in Jesus in general by all peoples."[2] He says:

> [Rabbinic Judaism] leaves atonement on the basis of law and good works and completely shuts out grace, which one sees in both the Hebrew Scriptures and New Testament. God becomes impersonal, and a nagging question persists as to where one finds Him.[3]

The late Arthur Kac, another Hebrew-Christian scholar and author, agreed. He wrote that under the system of Judaism established by the rabbis, "The word Jew has, among other things, come to mean opposition to Jesus Christ. Actually, since the first century much of Judaism developed as a reaction against Christianity." He quoted one Jewish writer who declared, "It is by the rejection of the Messiahship of Jesus that we proclaim to the world that we are still Jews."[4] I can tell you from my own experience that this is absolutely accurate.

HOPE FADES IN ISRAEL

For several decades, the Jews who remained in Israel held onto the hope that they would be able to expel the Romans and rebuild the Temple. But that hope faded with the failure of Simon Bar Kochba's war against the Romans in A.D. 132–136. Many thousands of Jews died in that rebellion, and most who survived were deported.

On the spot where the Temple had stood, Emperor Hadrian built a shrine to Jupiter. He also gave Jerusalem the Roman name of Aelia Capatolina and forbade Jews to live there. Any Jew who dared to enter Jerusalem did so at the risk of execution. The entire nation of Israel was officially renamed *Palaestina* in an attempt to obliterate all connections to the Jewish people.[5]

With the Temple gone, rabbinical interpretations of Scripture and Jewish law became increasingly important. Most likely beginning with the council in Yabneh, rabbis began to commit the oral law to writing, compiling what became known as the Mishnah.

Over the next few centuries, the Mishnah was further developed and a commentary on the commentary, called the Gemara, was also established. Together, these two works form the Talmud. The Torah, the Talmud and other rabbinic writings make up what is called Halakhah, the totality of Jewish law. Halakhah is filled with rules and practices that affect every area of a person's life. Observant Jews are told what to eat, what to wear, how to cut their hair, etc.

In his epic work, *The Life and Times of Jesus the Messiah,* the brilliant Jewish believer Alfred Edersheim wrote that the main difference between rabbinic Judaism and the teachings of Jesus is that rabbinic Judaism concerns itself with the outer man, while Jesus' teachings always focus on the inner man. "Rabbinism started with outward obedience and righteousness, and pointed toward sonship as its goal," he wrote. "The Gospel started with the free gift of forgiveness through faith and of sonship, and pointed to obedience and righteousness as its goal."[6] Edersheim writes that the differences between the teachings of the Talmud and the New Testament are not minor, but are "a total divergence . . . so that comparison between them is not possible."[7]

Even with such detailed rules, regulations and commands, there is still a great deal of disagreement and divergence among the various movements and sects within Judaism. We have a saying: "If you have two Jews, you will get three opinions." How true. It is difficult to get Jewish people to agree on much of anything, with the exception that a Jew cannot be Jewish and believe in Jesus.

TESHUVA VERSUS SACRIFICE

According to rabbinic Judaism, a Jew must take five steps to achieve forgiveness of sins. These steps are called *teshuva,* or return [to God]:

- Recognition of sin
- Remorse
- Desisting from sin
- Restitution
- Confession to God

Rabbi David R. Blumenthal, professor of Judaic Studies at Emory University in Atlanta, Georgia, explains:

> Rabbinic tradition teaches that all the steps to teshuva are necessary. . . . One may begin at any point—with action, analysis, remorse, restitution or confession. . . . As one cycles through the five phases of teshuva again and again, one's teshuva becomes more earnest, more serious. At its height, one achieves "full teshuva" (*Teshuvá gemurá*) which would require full consciousness and action such that, given the same situation, one would refrain from the sin for which one had repented.[8]

No one could argue that there is anything wrong with the five steps of teshuva. From a purely human viewpoint, they make a great deal of sense. But something is missing: the biblical requirement that the shedding of blood is absolutely essential to obtain forgiveness of sins.

Some rabbis even argue that the Hebrew Scriptures *never* make blood sacrifice a prerequisite for the forgiveness of sin. With all humility and respect, I wonder which Torah they have been reading. The Torah I read has numerous references to the connection between sacrifice and forgiveness. And as I stated earlier, every covenant or agreement that God made with man was literally *cut* with blood.

WHAT ABOUT TEFILLAH?

Tefillah, or "prayer," is the second of the three pillars of rabbinic Judaism. The word literally means "to attach oneself." The name speaks to the purpose of the ritual, which is to attach oneself to God. Jonathan Sacks, chief rabbi of Great Britain and the British Commonwealth, explains Tefillah this way:

> It is a movement from below, from man, reaching toward G-d. . . . [T]his is something appropriate to everyone and at every time. The Jewish soul has a bond with G-d. But it also inhabits a body, whose preoccupation with the material world may attenuate that bond. So it has constantly to be strengthened and renewed. This is the function of tefillah. And it is necessary for every Jew. For while there may be those who do not lack anything and thus have nothing to request of G-d, there is no-one who does not need to attach himself to the source of all life.[9]

What Rabbi Sacks says is true. Everyone must be attached to the one true God who is the Source of Life. As Yeshua said, "I am the vine; you are the branches. If a man remains in me and I in him, he will bear much fruit; apart from me you can do nothing" (John 15:5).

So what could possibly be wrong with prayer? Nothing, unless you are counting on your prayers to make you right with God. You could pray for 24 hours every day, and it would not make you righteous in God's eyes. God has made one provision for righteousness and forgiveness of sin. He has provided one final and eternal atonement for our souls: Yeshua, Jesus. He is the one and only way to right standing with the God of Israel.

So many people have a zeal for God, but not according to knowledge.

> For I can testify about them that they are zealous for God, but their zeal is not based on knowledge. Since they did not

know the righteousness that comes from God and sought
to establish their own, they did not submit to God's righteousness. Christ [Yeshua] is the end of the law so that there
may be righteousness for everyone who believes.

—ROMANS 10:2–4

It is bizarre that a Jewish person can believe in anything or
nothing and still be Jewish, but if he believes in Jesus, then he is no
longer Jewish. This is a spiritual issue, orchestrated by Satan himself
who has blinded their eyes to the truth. For as Yeshua said in John
14:6, "I am the way and the truth and the life. No one comes to the
Father except through me."

I say this with tears for my Jewish brothers and sisters all over
the world. It breaks my heart to see them searching in all the wrong
places for God to fill that aching void in their hearts, when I know
that the real answer is Yeshua, God's promised Messiah of Israel
and Savior of the world. I know that you who are reading this book
share this same burden with me. I implore you to reach out to that
Jewish person whom the Lord has placed in your life. He or she is
not there by accident. And above all, pray for him or her. Prayer
changes a person from within.

If you happen to be Jewish and have not yet accepted Yeshua
as your Messiah and Savior, He is waiting. All you need to do is ask
Him to come into your life and forgive you. He will. If you are not
yet sure if He is the Messiah and whether what you have read so far
is true or not, all you need to do is ask God to show you. He will,
as He did with me more than thirty years ago.

MITZVOT VERSUS SALVATION BY FAITH

As I stated earlier in this chapter, according to rabbinic Judaism
faithful Jews must follow 613 *mitzvot*, or commandments, 248

positive and 365 negative. Many mitzvot are rules that any moral person would obey, such as "Honor the old and wise," "Do not stand idly by when a human life is in danger," and "Do not afflict an orphan or a widow." Other mitzvot are impossible to carry out today because they concern acts of worship that are no longer applicable—the proper way to carry the Ark of the Covenant, for example, or the correct way to conduct various ceremonies in the Temple.

Who could possibly remember 613 laws, much less obey them? We who know Yeshua understand that when it comes to salvation or being made righteous, we do not have to! Only one thing is necessary for salvation, and that is to accept by faith the sacrifice Yeshua made on our behalf. Just as the animal sacrifice atoned for sin under the Mosaic Covenant, the blood of Yeshua—the final sacrifice—atones for the sins of those who believe in Him under the New Covenant. God knew we would never be able to keep the righteous standards of His law, and so He gave us the gift of grace through His Son.

As the apostle Paul writes in Ephesians 2:8–9:

> For it is by grace you have been saved, through faith—and this not from yourselves, it is the gift of God—not by works [Mitzvot or strict adherence to the law], so that no one can boast.

And as he also wrote in Galatians 2:15–16:

> We who are Jews by birth and not "Gentile sinners" know that a man is not justified by observing the law, but by faith in Jesus Christ [Yeshua the Messiah]. So we, too, have put our faith in [Yeshua the Messiah] that we may be justified by faith in [Messiah] and not by observing the law, because by observing the law no one will be justified.

So what does this say about the law? Does this mean that the law has been eradicated or that it no longer has any validity in our lives? Absolutely not! It is not the law itself that is bad—or even observance of the law. Rather, what is incorrect is the belief that we are justified by the law. No one can be justified, or made righteous, by the law. Paul says:

> But now a righteousness from God, apart from law, has been made known, to which the Law and the Prophets testify. This righteousness from God comes through faith in Jesus Christ to all who believe. There is no difference, for all have sinned and fall short of the glory of God, and are justified freely by his grace through the redemption that came by Christ Jesus. God presented him as a sacrifice of atonement, through faith in his blood. . . . [A] man is justified by faith apart from observing the law. . . . Do we, then, nullify the law by this faith? Not at all! Rather, we uphold the law.
>
> —ROMANS 3:21–25, 28, 31

No, the law has certainly not been removed. Jesus said, "Do not think that I have come to abolish the Law or the Prophets; I have not come to abolish them but to fulfill them" (Matthew 5:17).

What does Jesus mean when He says that He has come to "fulfill" the law and the prophets? A helpful way to understand what He means is to reverse the two syllables of the word and think of it as "fill full." Jesus came to "fill up to the fullest" the law and the prophets, like clean, fresh water being poured to the top of a glass until it overflows. Yeshua did not come to do away with the law, but rather to bring it into full meaning.

When Paul writes that we are no longer under the law, he is not saying that the law is bad. He is simply saying that our position in regard to the law has changed. What is this new position? Jeremiah 31:31–34 tells us that the law has been put in our minds and written in our hearts. So the law of God is still real in our lives, but we live it through the power of the Holy Spirit and are no longer under the condemnation of it. It is now internalized—it is in our hearts.

Many today espouse a conflict between grace and law that simply does not exist in Scripture. The idea that the Old Testament reveals a God of judgment, wrath and law and that the New Testament depicts a God of love and grace is simply an inaccurate dichotomy of the whole truth of Scripture from Genesis to Revelation. The Old Testament is filled with the grace, compassion and mercy of God, while the New Testament contains plenty of passages that demonstrate God's eternal law, righteous standard and judgment.

Take Ananias and Sapphira in Acts 5, for example. They were struck dead for telling lies in the presence of God. Does that sound like the God of the New Testament to you? And an example from the Old Testament is the whole sacrificial system, which was a demonstration of God's grace and mercy in providing a blood sacrifice, an atonement to cover the sins of His people, so that He could dwell among them.

Indeed, all of the atonements, laws, rules and regulations of the Old Covenant foreshadowed the ultimate atonement that God would provide at the appointed time—the atonement of Yeshua, the Messiah, His own Son—the Lamb of God created before the foundation of the world.

NO CERTAINTY IN RABBINIC JUDAISM

How much work must one do before he can be assured that he has been forgiven? Does a person need to perform just one more good deed? When a woman gives a check for $100 to help hungry children overseas, does God shake His head and say, "It should have been $200"? A person can find no comfort in a system of laws by which he or she must abide in order to be justified or made right with God. Not only is this true of Judaism, but it is the case with any other religions and cults. Many are based on a works-righteousness mentality. All of these, in essence, require us to *earn* our right standing with God or salvation.

Arthur Kac tells a moving story about the death of Rabbi Yochanan ben Zakkai, the father of rabbinic Judaism whom we discussed earlier in this chapter. Kac writes that when he was about to die, some of his disciples visited him and found him weeping. "Rabbi," they asked in astonishment, "do you weep—you, the light of Israel, the right-hand pillar of Judaism and the mighty interpreter of the Law?"

Riddled with uncertainty, the rabbi responded:

> Ah, my children, should I not weep if I were at this moment led before an earthly king, who may be in his grave tomorrow; whose anger, therefore, and the punishment he might inflict upon one could not last forever, and who moreover, might be moved to pity by words of entreaty, or be pacified with a gift? And you ask me why I weep, when I am being led into the presence of the Supreme King of kings, who lives throughout the countless ages of eternity; whose anger, therefore, and the punishment He may inflict upon me must last forever; who will not be moved by words of entreaty nor by the offer of a gift. Here are two ways before me, one leading to Paradise, and the other to Gehenna (hell), and I know not whither I am going.[10]

Throughout my childhood I believed there must be something more than this life, and from an early age I questioned why I was on this earth. I remember going to the rabbi and asking, "Rabbi, what happens after we die?"

Sitting back in his plush leather chair, the rabbi began to tell a story of a mountain climber working his way up a steep summit. "The mountain climber," said the rabbi, "cannot see what is over the hill because he is still climbing. God, on the other hand, dwells on top of the summit and sees beyond." I left the rabbi's office more confused than when I had entered.

After meeting God years later and understanding what the Bible really teaches, it occurred to me that the rabbi had no idea what happens after one dies. He was the rabbi—the man of great wisdom and authority—and so he had to give me an answer. But the truth was that he had no more idea about the afterlife than I did.

There is no certainty concerning the afterlife in Judaism. Nor is there any agreement on the subject. In fact, it may surprise you, but many Jews—even devout ones—are not even sure if there is a God, let alone an afterlife.

How different from the teachings of Yeshua the Messiah, who promises, "I tell you the truth, whoever hears my word and believes him who sent me has eternal life and will not be condemned; he has crossed over from death to life" (John 5:24). Yeshua was clear about where He was going—and where those who followed Him would be going. It is a place called "paradise" (Luke 23:43). Yeshua reassured His followers:

> In my Father's house are many rooms; if it were not so, I would have told you. I am going there to prepare a place for you. And . . . I will come back and take you to be with me that you also may be where I am.
> —John 14:2–3

With Yeshua, we have complete assurance.

How wonderful that we can know for certain what will happen after we pass from this life. For those who have yet to experience this, just keep an open mind and heart. As you read the Bible, you will see this promise with crystal clarity. All it takes is a step of educated faith to know for sure.

12

RESURRECTION: FACT OR FICTION?

Did Yeshua rise from the dead? For all of us, and most especially for Jews, the answer to this question makes all the difference.

The brilliant British philosopher John Locke (1632–1704) said,

> Our Savior's resurrection . . . is truly of great importance in Christianity; so great that His being or not being the Messiah stands or falls with it; so that these two important articles are inseparable and in effect make one. For since that time, believe one and you believe both; deny one of them, and you can believe neither.[1]

The apostle Paul wrote,

> And if Christ [Messiah] has not been raised, our preaching is useless and so is your faith. More than that, we are then found to be false witnesses about God, for we have testified about God that he raised Christ [Messiah] from the dead.
>
> —1 Corinthians 15:14–15

Five verses later Paul says emphatically, "But Christ [Messiah] has indeed been raised from the dead."

If Jesus cast off His graveclothes and walked out of His tomb, past the stone that had been rolled away, then that settles for all time the question "Who is Jesus of Nazareth?" He is undoubtedly Yeshua HaMashiach, Israel's Messiah.

I believe with all my heart that this is exactly what happened in that garden in Jerusalem nearly two thousand years ago. I believe because I myself have encountered the living Messiah—and because millions of other people around the world have also encountered Him—and as a result, our lives have changed forever. My faith, however, is not a blind faith. Abundant evidence both within and outside of Scripture validates a rational belief in the resurrection.

Sadly, I have talked to many of my Jewish brethren who are not aware of this evidence and tell me they simply cannot accept that something so miraculous could happen. The apostle Paul recognized and foresaw this when he said that the natural mind is at enmity with the things of God and must be transformed (see Romans 12:2) and when he said:

> For the message of the cross is foolishness to those who are perishing, but to us who are being saved it is the power of God. For it is written: "I will destroy the wisdom of the wise; the intelligence of the intelligent I will frustrate." . . . Jews

demand miraculous signs and Greeks look for wisdom, but we preach Christ [Messiah] crucified: a stumbling block to Jews and foolishness to Gentiles, but to those whom God has called, both Jews and Greeks, Christ [Messiah] the power of God and the wisdom of God.

—1 CORINTHIANS 1:18–19, 22–24

While we can present the rational arguments that overwhelmingly support Yeshua's resurrection from the dead, the Gospel, which holds the resurrection at its foundation, ultimately is spiritually discerned. A great battle rages in the heavenlies when a person's heart and mind engage in an inner battle over this spiritual, life-changing reality. For those of us who are believers, then, our greatest responsibility is to engage in that spiritual battle through the power of prayer. As I have said, prayer can change a person from the inside out. It releases the power of God upon him or her, and when that happens, revelation, faith and even transformation occur.

THREE WHO DID NOT BELIEVE

Many of the ancient Hebrew prophets pointed toward the Messiah's resurrection from the grave. But before I discuss their prophecies, I want to introduce you to three men who did not believe in the resurrection. The first of these is a gentleman by the name of C. S. Lewis (1898–1963).

Lewis was an atheist until he came face-to-face with the evidence that everything the New Testament says about Jesus is true—including the fact that He rose from the dead. He went on to become one of the foremost Christian apologists of the twentieth century, writing classic books such as *The Screwtape Letters*, *Mere Christianity* and *The Problem of Pain*, along with the well-known children's series *The Chronicles of Narnia*.

In the 1920s, while a student at Oxford University, Lewis wrote a letter to his father complaining about a religious revival that was taking place on campus. "But what can you do?" he wrote. "If you try to suppress it, you only make martyrs."[2]

Two years later he wrote to a friend named Owen Barfield,

> Terrible things are happening to me. The "Spirit" or "Real I" is showing an alarming tendency to become much more personal and is taking the offensive, and is behaving just like God. You'd better come on Monday at the latest or I may have entered a monastery.[3]

In his book *Surprised by Joy*, Lewis wrote of a college encounter with an atheist classmate:

> Early in 1926 the hardest boiled of all the atheists I ever knew sat in my room on the other side of the fire and remarked that the evidence for the historicity of the gospels was really surprisingly good. "Rum thing," he went on. "All that stuff about the Dying God. . . . It almost looks as if it had really happened once." If he, the cynic of cynics . . . were not . . . "safe," where could I turn? Was there . . . no escape?[4]

Lewis also said, "The [Christian] 'doctrines' are translations into our concepts and ideas of that which God has already expressed in language more adequate, namely the actual incarnation, crucifixion and resurrection."[5]

The second gentleman who did not believe in the resurrection is Frank Morison, an English journalist who set out to use his legal skills to prove that Yeshua's resurrection was a myth. He said:

> I wanted to take this last phase of the life of Jesus . . . to strip it of its overgrown primitive beliefs and dogmatic suppositions, and to see this supremely great person as he really was.[6]

Like Lewis before him, Morison began reading the Bible and studying the other evidence. He says he wanted to "sift some of the evidence at first hand, and to form [his] own judgment on the problems which it presents." The errors and contradictions he expected to find were not there. Instead:

> Things emerged from that old-world story which previously I should have thought impossible. Slowly but very definitely the conviction grew that the drama of those unforgettable weeks of human history was stranger and deeper than it seemed. . . . [L]ater . . . the irresistible logic of their meaning came into view.

Morison's research subsequently became a book, *Who Moved the Stone?*, a classic and well-regarded treatise filled with evidences for the truth of the resurrection.[7]

The third gentleman who was adamantly opposed to the truth of the resurrection is Lee Strobel, author of such bestselling books as *The Case for Christ, The Case for Faith, The Case for a Creator* and *The Case for Easter*. According to his online biography, Strobel received a law degree from Yale University in 1979. Following that, he worked as a journalist for fourteen years at *The Chicago Tribune* and other newspapers, where he won top honors for investigative reporting and public service journalism from United Press International.[8] Like Lewis and Morison before him, Strobel was an atheist.

Then he decided to use his highly regarded reporting skills to investigate the claims of Jesus. In *The Case for Easter*, Strobel writes that he knew that a belief in the resurrection was "the lynchpin" of faith in Jesus:

> Anyone can claim to be the Son of God. But if someone could substantiate that assertion by returning to life after being certifiably dead and buried—well, that would be a compelling

confirmation that he was telling the truth. Even for a skeptic like me. . . . As a reporter, I had seen lots of dead people—and none of them had ever come back to life. Christians could spin fanciful tales of an empty tomb, but they could never change the grim, absolute finality of death.[9]

Strobel spent much of two years studying the evidence for the resurrection and other claims of the New Testament.

As I began my investigation, three questions loomed: Was Jesus really dead after His ordeal on the cross? Was His tomb actually empty on that first Easter morning? And did credible people subsequently encounter Him?[10]

At the end of that time, Strobel was convinced beyond the shadow of a doubt that everything the New Testament says about Yeshua is true.

It is the same story, repeated so often before. The evidence of the resurrection of Yeshua always holds up to the scrutiny of sincere investigation if one seeks to find the truth without bias.

EXAMINING THE PROPHETIC EVIDENCE

So what is the evidence in favor of Yeshua's resurrection?

First, many prophecies in the Hebrew Scriptures point to the Messiah's death and resurrection. We have already discussed many of these in some detail, so I will not spend a great deal of time on them here. The best known of these is found in Isaiah 53:8–12:

By oppression and judgment he was taken away.
And who can speak of his descendants?
For he was cut off from the land of the living;
for the transgression of my people he was stricken.

He was assigned a grave with the wicked,
and with the rich in his death,
though he had done no violence,
nor was any deceit in his mouth.

Yet it was the LORD's will to crush him and cause him to
    suffer,
and though the LORD makes his life a guilt offering,
he will see his offspring and prolong his days,
and the will of the LORD will prosper in his hand.

After the suffering of his soul,
he will see the light of life and be satisfied;
by his knowledge my righteous servant will justify many,
and he will bear their iniquities.

Therefore I will give him a portion among the great,
and he will divide the spoils with the strong,
because he poured out his life unto death,
and was numbered with the transgressors.
For he bore the sin of many,
and made intercession for the transgressors.

How can someone be "cut off from the land of the living" and
then "see His offspring and prolong His days," or "see the light of
life and be satisfied"? There is only one answer: He returns to life
after death.

The same explanation is necessary to make sense of prophecies
in the book of Daniel. We previously discussed these words from
the ninth chapter:

Know therefore and understand, that from the going forth
of the commandment to restore and to build Jerusalem unto
the Messiah the Prince shall be seven weeks, and threescore
and two weeks: the street shall be built again, and the wall,
even in troublous times. And after threescore and two weeks

shall Messiah be cut off, but not for himself: and the people of the prince that shall come shall destroy the city and the sanctuary; and the end thereof shall be with a flood, and unto the end of the war desolations are determined.

—Daniel 9:25–26, kjv

When Daniel says that the Messiah will "be cut off, but not for himself," he means that He will die, not because of anything He has done, but because of what others have done. In other words, Messiah will die for the sins of people like you and me. And yet, Daniel also says of Messiah:

In my vision . . . there before me was one like a son of man, coming with the clouds of heaven. He approached the Ancient of Days and was led into his presence. He was given authority, glory and sovereign power; all peoples, nations and men of every language worshiped him. His dominion is an everlasting dominion that will not pass away, and his kingdom is one that will never be destroyed.

—Daniel 7:13–14

Again, the Messiah dies and yet reigns forever in a Kingdom that will never end. How can both of these seemingly diametrically opposed prophecies be true? The only explanation is a resurrection from the dead.

Over and over the prophets repeat the theme of triumph coming from defeat. The psalmist says, "God will redeem my life from the grave; he will surely take me to himself" (Psalm 49:15). He also says, "The stone the builders rejected has become the capstone; the Lord has done this, and it is marvelous in our eyes" (Psalm 118:22–23).

And Zechariah writes:

And I will pour out on the house of David and the inhabitants of Jerusalem a spirit of grace and supplication. They will

look on me, the one they have pierced, and they will mourn
for him as one mourns for an only child, and grieve bitterly for
him as one grieves for a firstborn son. . . . On that day a fountain will be opened to the house of David and the inhabitants
of Jerusalem, to cleanse them from sin and impurity.

—ZECHARIAH 12:10; 13:1

After reading prophetic passages like these, it makes no sense
to say that the Hebrew Scriptures never spoke of the Messiah dying
and then rising from the dead. Clearly, they did.

EXAMINING THE HISTORICAL EVIDENCE

When Paul was on trial before Herod Agrippa, he said, "The king
is familiar with these things, and I can speak freely to him. I am
convinced that none of this has escaped his notice, because it was
not done in a corner" (Acts 26:26).

This is one of the most compelling evidences for belief in the
resurrection of Jesus. It did not happen "once upon a time" or "a long
time ago in a galaxy far, far away." It happened at a specific place and
time, Jerusalem, during the celebration of Passover, around A.D. 30.
Because it is so specific, it should be fairly easy to disprove if it were
not true. And yet, no one has ever been able to disprove it, not even
people such as Herod Agrippa who lived in Jerusalem at the time
and were opposed to the spread of faith in Yeshua.

Suppose I write a book about Elvis Presley in which I claim
that he had been raised from the dead. Do you think anyone would
believe me (outside of a few people who get their information from
The National Enquirer)? Of course not. Even though Presley has
been dead for decades, many people remember him and know that
he did not come back from the grave. Similarly, when the New
Testament was written, many people who had been alive during
the time Yeshua lived and was crucified were still in Israel. If they

knew that He had never come out of that tomb they would have said so, and the newly birthed movement of His followers would have instantly crumbled.

Now, I am not trying for a minute to equate Jesus of Nazareth with Elvis Presley, except to show that you cannot get away with making up wild stories about people—even if they have been gone for thirty years or more. In the first few decades after Yeshua's resurrection, no one ever tried to claim that the story was pure fiction. Even the Jewish leaders who were opposed to Him admitted that *something* strange had happened. So instead of denying the entire story, they accused His disciples of stealing His body.

What they did not acknowledge was that this would have been impossible, since guards were posted at the tomb to make sure this did not happen. Besides, the tomb was sealed with a stone that could not be moved without the combined effort of several strong men. Nobody could have sneaked into the cemetery, snatched the body and made a quick getaway.

In *Who Moved the Stone?*, Frank Morison addresses the question of the stone from a historical perspective. He writes that when Mary and her friends visited the tomb on that morning following Shabbat:

> The question as to how they were to remove this stone must . . . have been a source of considerable perplexity to the women. . . . The stone, which is known to have been large and of considerable weight, was their great difficulty. When, therefore, we find in the earliest record, the Gospel of Mark, the words "Who will roll away the stone from the entrance of the tomb?" (Mark 16:13), we can hardly avoid feeling that this preoccupation of the women with the question of the stone is not only a psychological necessity of the problem, but a definitely historical element in the situation right up to the moment of their arrival at the grave. . . . [This stone is] the one silent and infallible witness in the whole episode.[11]

Wilbur Smith, a college professor who wrote a bestselling book titled *Therefore Stand,* also investigated the resurrection's historical validity. He wrote:

> The meaning of the resurrection is a theological matter, but the face of the resurrection is a historical matter; the nature of the resurrection of the body of Jesus may be a mystery, but the fact that the body disappeared from the tomb is a matter to be decided upon by historical evidence. . . . The place is of geographical definiteness . . . that tomb was made out of rock in a hillside near Jerusalem, and was not composed of some mythological gossamer, or cloud-dust, but is something which has geographical significance. The guards put before that tomb were not aerial beings from Mt. Olympus; the Sanhedrin was a body of men meeting frequently in Jerusalem. As a vast mass of literature tells us, this person, Yeshua, was a living person, a man among men, whatever else He was . . . Let it simply be said that we know more about the details of the hours immediately before and the actual death of Jesus, in and near Jerusalem, than we know about the death of any other one man in all the ancient world.[12]

Noted Roman Catholic theologian Raymond E. Brown agrees:

> Jesus was buried in a certain place. If that place was known, it could have been visited at a certain time. If the tomb was visited and it contained the skeleton, or corpse, of Jesus, it is difficult, if not impossible, to understand how the disciples could have preached that God raised Jesus from the dead, since there would have been irrefutable evidence that he had not done so.[13]

Brown also finds evidence for the resurrection in the fact that non-believing Jews of the first century never challenged the story that the tomb had been empty just three days after the crucifixion. "Our earliest traces of Jewish apologetics against the resurrection do not reject the empty tomb; they explain that the body was taken away by the disciples or someone else." He cites an early legend in which the gardener removed and disposed of the body of Jesus because he did not want crowds coming to visit the tomb and trampling his vegetables.[14]

EXAMINING THE EVIDENCE OF THE WITNESSES

According to eyewitness accounts, for forty days after His resurrection Jesus appeared to dozens of witnesses. He appeared to Mary Magdalene at the tomb (see John 20:10–18). He visited with Cleopas and another disciple on the road to Emmaus (see Luke 24:13–32). He showed Himself to His apostles on several occasions (see Luke 24:36–43; John 20:26–28; John 21:1–14). This may be the most compelling evidence of all. The New Testament says that when the resurrected Jesus first appeared to them, they were cowering behind closed doors, a brokenhearted group afraid of both the Romans and the Jewish leaders. After learning that Jesus had returned to life, they were ready to change the world—and did.

But it gets better:

> After that, he appeared to more than five hundred of
> the brothers at the same time, most of whom are still living,
> though some have fallen asleep. Then he appeared to James,
> then to all the apostles, and last of all he appeared to me (Paul)
> also, as to one abnormally born.
> —1 CORINTHIANS 15:6–8

In our discussion of the historical evidence, we mentioned that when the gospels were written, Yeshua's resurrection was still open to investigation, since many people who had lived then were still alive. The same applies here. When Paul wrote this passage in 1 Corinthians 15, many of those who had seen the resurrected Jesus were still alive and could have been questioned regarding what they had seen. Imagine a court case in which more than five hundred witnesses showed up to testify for the defense? The prosecution would not have the slightest chance of winning the case.

In *The Case for Easter,* Lee Strobel says:

> Without question, the amount of testimony and corroboration of Jesus' post-resurrection appearances is staggering. To put it into perspective, if you were to call each one of the witnesses to a court of law to be cross-examined for just fifteen minutes each, and you went around the clock without a break, it would take you from breakfast on Monday until dinner on Friday to hear them all. After listening to 129 straight hours of eyewitness testimony, who could possibly walk away unconvinced?[15]

Strobel also quotes Scottish scholar and theologian John Drane:

> The earliest evidence we have for the resurrection goes back almost to the time immediately after the resurrection. . . . This is the evidence contained in the early sermons in the Acts of the Apostles.[16]

Drane is referring to passages such as these:

> God has raised this Jesus to life, and we are all witnesses of the fact.
> —Acts 2:32

> You killed the author of life, but God raised him from the dead. We are witnesses of this.
> —Acts 3:15

For many days he was seen by those who had traveled with him from Galilee to Jerusalem. They are now his witnesses to our people.

—ACTS 13:31

The overwhelming evidence of the many witnesses to Jesus' resurrection is another arrow in the quiver of irrefutable truth.

EXAMINING THE MEDICAL EVIDENCE

Some attempt to discredit belief in the resurrection by arguing that Jesus was not dead when He was taken down from the cross. They argue that He had merely fainted or "swooned" and quickly recovered in the cool darkness of the tomb.

To answer this challenge, we will consider John's eyewitness report of Jesus' death. John writes:

> Because the Jews did not want the bodies left on the crosses during the Sabbath, they asked Pilate to have the legs broken and the bodies taken down. The soldiers therefore came and broke the legs of the first man who had been crucified with Jesus, and then those of the other. But when they came to Jesus and found that he was already dead, they did not break his legs. Instead, one of the soldiers pierced Jesus' side with a spear, bringing a sudden flow of blood and water. The man who saw it has given testimony, and his testimony is true. He knows that he tells the truth, and he testifies so that you also may believe.
>
> —JOHN 19:31–35

In the above passage, John gives a careful eyewitness account of the Messiah's final moments. He did not set out to argue with those who claim that Jesus did not die on the cross but merely fainted; yet when he describes the water and blood that came out of Jesus' side, he gives irrefutable evidence that the crucified One was already dead.

According to experts like Dr. Alexander Metherell, M.D., Ph.D., Jesus died of heart failure. "Even before he died," Metherell says in an interview with Lee Strobel,

> the hypovolemic shock would have caused a . . . rapid heart rate that would have contributed to heart failure, resulting in the collection of fluid in the membrane around the heart . . . as well as around the lungs.[17]

John's description of what flowed out of Jesus' body when the spear pierced it reveals that the spear passed through a lung and into His heart. When it was withdrawn, the doctor explains, a clear, watery fluid would have flowed out of the wound, followed by "a large volume of blood."[18] Metherell concludes that "the spear thrust into [Jesus'] heart would have settled the issue once and for all. And the Romans were not about to risk their own deaths by allowing Him to walk away alive."[19]

Drs. Brad Harrub and Bert Thompson agree with Metherell's assessment:

> Much speculation has centered on the exact location of the puncture wound and thus the source of the resulting blood and water. However, the Greek word (*pleura*) that John used clearly denotes the area of the intercoastal ribs that cover the lungs. Given the upward angle of the spear, and the thoracic location of the wound, abdominal organs can be ruled out as having provided the blood and water. A more likely scenario would suggest that the piercing affected a lung (along with any built-up fluid), the pericardial sac surrounding the heart, the right atrium of the heart itself, the pulmonary vessels, and/or the aorta. . . . [T]he blood could have resulted from the heart, the aorta, or any of the pulmonary vessels. Water probably was

provided by pleural or pericardial fluids (that surround the lungs and heart).[20]

In addition, Pilate had Jesus scourged before delivering Him over to be crucified. Often, the scourging alone would result in death. And Jesus' flogging was worse than usual, since Pilate apparently hoped to win some sympathy for Jesus by showing the crowd how badly He had been beaten (see John 19:1–6). Jesus surely lost a great deal of blood during His flogging, which would have resulted in lowered blood pressure and shock, and which in turn would cause irreversible cell and organ damage—and eventually death.

An article in the *Journal of the American Medical Association* also concluded that Jesus was dead when His body was removed from the cross. Portions of this article are reprinted below:

> Two aspects of Jesus' death have been the source of great controversy, namely, the nature of the wound in His side and the cause of His death after only several hours on the cross. . . . [T]he Greek word (*pleura*) used by John clearly denoted laterality and often implied the ribs. Therefore, it seems probable that the wound was in the thorax. . . .
>
> [T]he water probably represented serous pleural and pericardial fluid. . . . The blood, in contrast, may have originated from the right atrium or the right ventricle or perhaps from a hemopericardium.
>
> Jesus' death after only three to six hours on the cross surprised even Pontius Pilate. The fact that Jesus cried out in a loud voice and then bowed His head and died suggests the possibility of a catastrophic terminal event. . . .
>
> However, another explanation may be more likely. Jesus' death may have been hastened simply by his state of exhaustion and by the severity of the scourging. . . .
>
> [T]he important feature may be not how he died but rather if he died. Clearly, the weight of historical and medical evidence indicates that Jesus was dead before the wound to His

side was inflicted. . . . [I]nterpretations based on the assump-
tion that Jesus did not die on the cross appear to be at odds
with modern medical knowledge.[21]

I realize that this medical analysis is a bit complex, but it certainly shows that medical science agrees that Jesus died on that
cross.

CHALLENGES TO THE RESURRECTION

I have only scratched the surface of the voluminous evidence in
support of the resurrection. Now I want to take just a few moments
to discuss some of the challenges that have been raised by skeptics
in recent years.

The Plot Theory

In 1965, Hugh Schonfield (1901–1988) wrote *The Passover Plot*,
in which he claimed that Jesus had orchestrated His own crucifixion and resurrection. Schonfield, who authored more than forty
books, was a Jew who called himself "a Nazarene." Even though he
believed that Yeshua was indeed the Messiah, at one point in his life
he did not believe in the resurrection. *The Passover Plot* was by far
his bestselling book, and was made into a movie in 1976 starring
Zalman King.

Schonfield alleged that Jesus arranged it so that He would have
to spend "only" a few hours on the cross. He says this almost as
if a short crucifixion would not be much worse than a long walk
on the beach. But he vastly underestimates the deadly power of
crucifixion.

Josephus, the Jewish historian who served in the Roman army,
recorded an incident when he tried to rescue some acquaintances
who were being crucified:

And when I was sent by Titus Caesar with Cerealins, and a thousand horsemen, to a certain village called Thecoa . . . saw many captives crucified, and remembered three of them as my former acquaintances. I was very sorry at this in my mind, and went with tears in my eyes to Titus, and told him of them; so he immediately commanded them to be taken down, and to have the greatest care taken of them, in order to their recovery; yet two of them died under the physician's hand, while the third recovered.[22]

Crucifixion was deadly, especially when preceded by a vicious flogging. Schonfield's theory just does not hold water.

The Swoon Theory

According to this theory, Jesus merely lapsed into unconsciousness on the cross. When His broken body was placed in the cool, dark tomb, He recovered. We have already discussed this in some detail and have seen how medical science stands against it.

In his book, *Evidence That Demands a Verdict*, Josh McDowell quotes Bishop E. LeCamus of La Rochelle, France, as saying that if Jesus were alive when taken from the cross, He most certainly would have died in the tomb, "as the contact of the body with the cold stone of the sepulchre would have been enough to bring on a syncope through the congelation of the blood, owing to the fact that the regular circulation was already checked." He goes on to say that a man who has fainted is not revived by being shut up in a cave, but rather, by being exposed to open air.[23]

If Jesus had managed to survive, He would have been a broken shell of a man due to the torture He had endured, and not a heroic figure who inspired His disciples to conquer the world on His behalf. For this reason alone, the "swoon theory" does not make sense.

The Theft Theory

The theft theory was put forward by Jesus' opponents in the days immediately following the resurrection, and it is still around today. Matthew 28:11–15 says that after the resurrection:

> Some of the guards went into the city and reported to the chief priests everything that had happened. When the chief priests had met with the elders and devised a plan, they gave the soldiers a large sum of money, telling them, "You are to say, 'His disciples came during the night and stole him away while we were asleep.' If this report gets to the governor, we will satisfy him and keep you out of trouble." So the soldiers took the money and did as they were instructed. And this story has been widely circulated among the Jews to this very day.

The story the guards were paid to tell certainly has some holes in it. If they were asleep, for example, how did they know that Jesus' disciples came and stole His body? And is it logical to believe that two (or more) guards would have fallen asleep at the same time, considering that falling asleep while on guard duty was punishable by death? Furthermore, would they not have awakened when they heard that huge stone being rolled away?

Still, the story persists. Justin Martyr's *Dialogue With Trypho*, written around A.D. 150, is the record of an extended conversation between Justin, a believer in Jesus, and Trypho, a Jewish nonbeliever. At one point, Trypho is quoted as talking about "Jesus, a Galilean deceiver, whom we crucified; but His disciples stole Him by night from the tomb . . . and now deceive men by asserting that He has risen from the dead and ascended into heaven."[24]

The most amazing thing about these theories is that they openly admit that Jesus' body was missing from the tomb. The debate is not about the disappearance of His body, but rather about how it disappeared.

The Hallucination Theory

The people who thought this one up decided that all those who saw Jesus after His resurrection were actually hallucinating. The theory purports that His followers wanted so badly to see Him alive again that they suffered from mass hysteria.

But even if this theory were a possibility—which it is not—it does not explain what happened with the apostle Thomas. The Bible says that Thomas was not present the first time the risen Messiah revealed Himself to the apostles. When the others told Thomas what had happened he quite understandably refused to believe them. He replied, "Unless I see the nail marks in his hands and put my finger where the nails were, and put my hand into his side, I will not believe it" (John 20:25).

John continues:

> A week later his disciples were in the house again, and Thomas was with them. Though the doors were locked, Jesus came and stood among them and said, "Peace be with you!" Then he said to Thomas, "Put your finger here; see my hands. Reach out your hand and put it into my side. Stop doubting and believe." Thomas said to him, "My Lord and my God!"
> —John 20:26–28

Obviously, Thomas could not have put his hand into the side of a hallucination.

But even if one does not accept this Scripture, there are many other reasons to disregard the hallucination theory. We have already seen that Jesus appeared to more than five hundred people after His resurrection. Josh McDowell quotes Professor Thomas J. Thorburn on this:

> It is absolutely inconceivable that as many as five hundred persons . . . should experience all kinds of sensuous

impressions—visual, auditory, tactual—and that all these manifold experiences should rest entirely upon subjective hallucination. We say that this is incredible, because if such a theory were applied to any other than a "supernatural" event in history, it would be dismissed forthwith as a ridiculously insufficient explanation.[25]

In the *Christian Research Journal*, Gary Habermas, chairman of the department of philosophy and theology at Liberty University, gives a few other reasons why the hallucination theory does not work. He writes:

> The wide variety of times and places when Jesus appeared, along with the differing mindsets of the witnesses, is simply a huge obstacle. Men and women, hard-headed and soft-hearted alike, all believing that they saw Jesus, both indoors and outdoors, by itself provides an insurmountable barrier for hallucinations.[26]

Habermas cites other objections, such as the fact that hallucinations do not change lives but Jesus' disciples were transformed by seeing their risen Master.

Finally, if Jesus' appearances were hallucinations, why did they suddenly stop after forty days? They should have continued to spread to other believers.

The Wrong Tomb Theory

This is the most ridiculous of all the attempts to explain away the resurrection, and yet it has been used for centuries. Proponents say that Mary Magdalene simply got confused when she went to the tomb on that resurrection morning and wound up at the wrong location. Yes, the tomb was empty, they say, but it was not Jesus' tomb.

But what about Peter and John? Did they go to the wrong tomb, too? If they did, surely Joseph of Arimathea would have set them straight. After all, it was his tomb, so he certainly would have known where it was. This theory does not explain the origin of the grave clothes folded neatly in the tomb, or the angel who announced, "He is not here; He has risen" (Matthew 28:6).

When I look at history and see how many billions have believed in Yeshua—how His life and death transformed time itself—I have to ask how anyone could ever believe all this happened just because Mary went to the wrong tomb. Such a "theory" is ridiculous!

THE EVIDENCE IS CONCLUSIVE

Regarding the overwhelming evidence in support of the resurrection, attorney and author Sir Edward Clarke said, "As a lawyer I have made a prolonged study of the evidences for the events of the first Easter Day. To me the evidence is conclusive, and over and over again in the High Court I have secured the verdict on evidence not nearly so compelling."[27]

I will close this discussion on the resurrection by repeating the following words of the apostle Paul:

> And if Christ [Messiah] has not been raised, our preaching is useless and so is your faith. . . . [F]or we have testified about God that he raised Christ [Messiah] from the dead. But he did not raise him if in fact the dead are not raised. For if the dead are not raised, then Christ [Messiah] has not been raised either. And if Christ [Messiah] has not been raised, your faith is futile; you are still in your sins. . . . But Christ [Messiah] has indeed been raised from the dead. . . . For since death came through a man, the resurrection of the dead comes also through a man.
>
> —1 CORINTHIANS 15:14–17, 20–21

Yes, Yeshua was indeed raised from the dead and promises that if we put our faith in Him, we also will be resurrected into newness of life in the world to come. I hope that the evidence I have mentioned in this chapter will help to strengthen your belief in Yeshua as the risen Messiah, for His resurrection is truly a cornerstone of our faith.

13

EVIDENCE FOR THE VIRGIN BIRTH

What about the virgin birth of the Messiah? Is it important? Does it really matter?

The answer to both questions is yes. I love the way the theologian Carl F. H. Henry put it. He called the virgin birth the

> essential, historical indication of the Incarnation, bearing not only an analogy to the divine and human natures of the Incarnate, but also bringing out the nature, purpose, and bearing of this work of God to salvation.[1]

In other words, the virgin birth is essential to the incarnation of God (God in human form) and the Messiahship of Yeshua.

THE BIBLICAL CASE FOR THE VIRGIN BIRTH

In order to make a biblical case for the virgin birth, we have to go all the way back to Genesis 3:15. In the Garden of Eden, when God asked Adam and Eve why they disobeyed Him and ate of the Tree of Knowledge of Good and Evil, Adam pointed at Eve, and Eve pointed at the serpent. The Bible says:

> The LORD God said to the serpent,
> "Because you have done this,
> Cursed are you more than all cattle,
> and more than every beast of the field;
> On your belly you will go,
> and dust you will eat
> all the days of your life;
>
> "And I will put enmity
> between you and the woman,
> and between *your seed and her seed*;
> he shall bruise you on the head,
> and you shall bruise him on the heel."
> —GENESIS 3:14–15, NASB, EMPHASIS MINE

Man disobeyed God's one directive and in so doing brought a condition of separation between himself and his Creator. We are suffering the consequences of that decision to this very day. But in the midst of this sad chapter in human history, God promised a glimmer of hope when He declared, "I will put enmity between you and the woman, and between *your seed and her seed*; he shall bruise you on the head, and you shall bruise him on the heel" (Genesis 3:15, NASB). The rabbis of old understood this to be a promise of redemption. In fact, Adam and Eve were hoping that Cain would be this redeemer. To their grave disappointment, Cain turned out to be a murderer.

The point I want to make here is that Genesis 3:15 specifically refers to the seed of a woman. What is strange about this is that physiologically the seed comes through the man in the act of procreation, whereas the woman provides the egg. But here, Scripture specifically states that the seed of the woman ultimately will bring redemption.

The rabbis of old have understood this passage to be speaking of Messiah's triumph over evil. This is why "Seed of the Woman" became one of the titles of the coming Messiah. From the beginning of time and throughout Jewish history, then, the prophecy of the virgin birth was essential to the Jewish Messiah.

ELEVATING THE STATUS OF WOMEN

The title "Seed of the Woman" takes on even more significance when we consider that Jewish society in Old Testament times was completely male-dominated. It was not uncommon for men to have several wives. The family estate passed to the sons, not the daughters—and especially to the firstborn son. I believe that in bringing the Messiah into the world through the seed of a woman, God was elevating the status of women everywhere and for all time. This says something important about the dignity and status of women that all men would do well to recognize.

THE CONTINUATION OF THE SIN NATURE

An interesting theory that is worth mentioning concerns the continuation of the sin nature. It is believed by some that man's sin nature since the Fall [of man] was passed down through the DNA of the male. Being born of a virgin, the Messiah bypassed the sin nature, and therefore was able to be born without sin and live a sinless life. I am not stating this as fact but simply as a possible explanation.

Whether it is true or not, it illustrates another important reason for the virgin birth: In order for Yeshua to pay the penalty for our sins, He had to be without sin Himself.

THE PROPHECIES OF ISAIAH

Another explicit prophecy of Messiah's virgin birth is found in Isaiah 7:14: "Therefore the Lord himself will give you a sign: The virgin will be with child and will give birth to a son, and will call him Immanuel."

I will admit that this verse is highly controversial and has been a source of continual disagreement between rabbis and Christian apologists for centuries. The fight is over the Hebrew word here that is interpreted "virgin." The word used in the Hebrew text no less than six times is *almah* (הַמְלֹצ). It is used, for example, in Genesis 24:43 to describe Isaac's future wife, Rebekah, where it is translated "maiden," "young maiden" or "maiden of marriageable age." Jewish leaders who refuse to acknowledge Yeshua as Messiah claim that this word has been mistranslated and clearly means "young maiden," rather than "virgin." Such leaders argue that if Isaiah wanted to say "virgin," he would have used the Hebrew word *betulah* (בתולה), which clearly means "virgin" rather than *almah*.

Yet when the Old Testament was translated into Greek in 250 B.C. to provide a readable text for the language of the day, the Jewish translators chose to use the Greek word *parthenos*, which definitely means "virgin." Contrary to what some falsely teach, this is not a late Christian insertion into the Hebrew Scriptures, as it was translated 250 years before Yeshua [Jesus] was ever born.

Furthermore, there are a number of reasons why use of the word *virgin* makes sense. First, scholars agree that the word *almah* refers exclusively to a woman who is not married. If the woman to whom Isaiah refers in this passage is unmarried and pregnant by natural—as opposed to supernatural—means, then she is guilty of immorality. And if this were true, how could the birth of her son fit the criteria of being "a sign from God"? Isaiah is talking about a godly woman who is pregnant although she is not married. Under the Law of Moses, fornication was a serious matter, and neither fornicators nor children born outside of wedlock were highly regarded, as we will see later in this chapter. The mother of the Messiah simply cannot be a godly woman unless she is a virgin, impregnated by supernatural means.

Another problem for those who contend that Isaiah was not referring to a virgin birth is that the ordinary birth of a child could hardly be regarded as a great sign from God. After all, thousands of children are born every day. Please do not misunderstand what I am saying. I believe the birth of every child is a miracle, and I am a proud papa who loves his children more than I could possibly express. But Isaiah was giving a prophecy regarding the coming of the Messiah who would save the Jewish people. For the birth of such a child to be a sign from God, there would have to be something special and unusual about it. It most certainly would not be an average birth simply of a married woman who happened to be young.

At the time the virgin prophecy in Isaiah was given, Israel was at the mercy of its enemies. God was saying that He had not forgotten His people. He was encouraging them that these dark days would pass, the Deliverer would come, and the Light would shine in the darkness. The only explanation that accurately fits this prophecy is that this was talking about the Messiah who would be born of a virgin as a sign of God's faithfulness. Yeshua fulfilled this prophecy some seven hundred years later.

Matthew is clear in his understanding that Yeshua is the one to whom Isaiah was referring:

This is how the birth of [Yeshua, the Messiah] came about: his mother Mary was pledged to be married to Joseph, but before they came together, she was found to be with child through the Holy Spirit. Because Joseph her husband was a righteous man and did not want to expose her to public disgrace, he had in mind to divorce her quietly.

But after he had considered this, an angel of the Lord appeared to him in a dream and said, "Joseph son of David, do not be afraid to take Mary home as your wife, because what is conceived in her is from the Holy Spirit. She will give birth to a son, and you are to give him the name [Yeshua], because he will save his people from their sins."

All this took place to fulfill what the Lord had said through the prophet [Isaiah]: "The virgin will be with child and will give birth to a son, and they will call him Immanuel"—which means, "God with us."

—MATTHEW 1:18–23

The name *Immanuel* in Hebrew means "God with us" (עִמָּנוּאֵל). It is symbolic of the prophetic name of the Messiah, prophesying that He would be born of a virgin and would be "God with us." A vital aspect of Isaiah's prophecy, it is, I believe, to be taken literally. The child to whom Isaiah refers will be God in the flesh come to earth to live among His people. Isaiah confirms this two chapters later, when he says:

> For to us a child is born,
> to us a son is given,
> and the government will be on his shoulders.
> And he will be called
> Wonderful Counselor, Mighty God,
> Everlasting Father, Prince of Peace.
>
> Of the increase of his government and peace
> there will be no end.
> He will reign on David's throne

and over his kingdom,
establishing and upholding it
with justice and righteousness
from that time on and forever.
The zeal of the LORD Almighty
will accomplish this.

—ISAIAH 9:6–7

Some have said that Isaiah's prophecy was merely referring to a child who was about to be born, perhaps to Ahaz. The eleventh-century rabbi Rashi, whom we have discussed previously, said that this verse applied to Isaiah's own son, *Maher shalal hash baz* (see Isaiah 8:1). But the prophecy of the name *Emmanuel* proves that this theory does not make sense. *Maher shalal hash baz* means "the spoil hurries, the prey speeds along," which is not quite the same as "God with us." And in addition to this, no child born in the time of Isaiah fits the prophecy he gave. No child established an everlasting government that brought peace to the world. And no prophet of God would refer to a mere human being as "Mighty God" or "Everlasting Father."

EARLY BELIEFS ABOUT THE VIRGIN BIRTH

The virgin birth is mentioned directly only twice in the New Testament—once in Matthew 1, and again in Luke 1. Although it is alluded to in other passages—such as Galatians 4:4—it is not given a tremendous amount of attention.

And yet the evidence shows that from the beginning it was an important tenet of New Covenant faith. Early references to the virgin birth are found in the writings of Aristides, A.D. 125; Justin Martyr, A.D. 150; and Tertullian, A.D. 200,[2] to mention just a few. Furthermore, one New Testament passage indicates that certain Pharisees who opposed Yeshua had heard the stories of the virgin birth and therefore attacked Him as being an illegitimate child. It was a desperate attempt to destroy His credibility among the people, but it did not work. John 8 tells of this heated encounter between Jesus and a group of Pharisees:

> "If you were Abraham's children," said Jesus, "then you would do the things Abraham did. As it is, you are determined to kill me, a man who has told you the truth that I heard from God. Abraham did not do such things. You are doing the things your own father does."
>
> —JOHN 8:39–41

This angered the Pharisees so greatly that they ridiculed Jesus: "We are not illegitimate children," they protested. "The only Father we have is God himself" (John 8:41). In other words, they were accusing Yeshua of being illegitimately born. The King James Version uses harsher language: "Then said they to him, 'We be not born of fornication [like you]; we have one Father, even God.' " In calling Jesus "a bastard," the Pharisees were doing more than mocking Him. They were reminding Him of what the Torah says: "A mamzer shall not enter into the assembly of Adonai, nor may his descendants down to the tenth generation enter the assembly of Adonai" (Deuteronomy 23:2, The Torah). *Mamzer* is the Hebrew word for "bastard," which means "polluted."

Even at that early date, it was being circulated among the leadership that there was something different about the birth of this Teacher from Nazareth. Derogatory reports and lies began to propagate, as these leaders felt more and more threatened by His growing authority. These lies then made their way into the Talmud, where Yeshua is called *Ye'shu ben Pandera*, or the illegitimate son of a Roman soldier named Pandera. Talmudic scholar Peter Schafer writes, "The Talmud seems to be convinced that [Jesus'] true father was Pandera, his mother's lover, and that he was a bastard in the full sense of the word." The Babylonian Talmud also portrays Mary as a brazen woman who grew her hair long and went out with it unfastened, a sure "indication of her indecent behavior."[3] In other words, the Talmud claims that Jesus is not only the illegitimate son of a brazen woman but is also a Gentile—and even worse, a Roman, a member of the government that has oppressed the Jewish nation for so long.

The authors of these stories were not interested in the facts. Instead, they were attacking Yeshua with the intent of destroying His credibility so as to establish once and for all that He could not be the Messiah. Yet such statements prove that the virgin birth was widely known in the first few centuries after Yeshua's death.

WITH GOD, ALL THINGS ARE POSSIBLE

Some people say the virgin birth cannot be true because the concept violates the laws of biology. What they are unable to see is that God is the architect of those laws, and He can bend them at any time and in any way He desires.

In *The Case for Faith*, Lee Strobel interviews Dr. William Lane Craig, who has written numerous books, including *In Defense of Miracles* and *The Intellectuals Speak Out about God*. Dr. Craig has excellent credentials, including doctorates in philosophy from the University of Birmingham in England and in theology from the University of Munich.

When Strobel asked Dr. Craig how a man of such intellect and learning was able to believe in the virgin birth, Dr. Craig replied:

> It is funny you should ask specifically about the virgin birth, because that was a major stumbling block to my becoming a Christian [believer]. I thought it was totally absurd. . . . When the [Gospel] message was first shared with me as a teenager, I had already studied biology. I knew that for the

virgin birth to be true, a Y chromosome had to be created out of Mary's ovum, because Mary did not possess the genetic material to produce a male child. To me, this was utterly fantastic. It just did not make sense.

What happened to change Dr. Craig's mind?

I sort of put that issue aside and became a [believer] anyway, even though I did not really believe in the virgin birth. But then, after becoming a [believer], it occurred to me that if I really do believe in a God who created the universe, then for him to create a Y chromosome would be child's play.[4]

When Strobel pressed him on the issue, Dr. Craig added:

I guess the authenticity of the Person of Jesus and the truth of His message were so powerful that they simply overwhelmed any residual doubts that I had. . . . You do not need to have all your questions answered to come to faith. You just have to say, "The weight of the evidence seems to show this is true, so even though I do not have answers to all my questions, I am going to believe and hope for answers in the long run." That is what happened with me.[5]

Strobel writes that as he finished his interview with Dr. Craig, he reflected upon how his relationship with Jesus had changed his own life:

Based on how God has transformed my life, my attitudes, my relationships, my motivations, my marriage and my priorities through His very real ongoing presence in my life, I realized at that moment that miracles like manna from heaven, the virgin birth and the resurrection—well, in the end they are child's play for a God like that.[6]

Lee Strobel is exactly right. We serve a God of miracles. He is sovereign. If He created the heavens and the earth out of the void, light out of darkness and man from the dust of the earth, then nothing is too hard for Him—certainly not a virgin birth or a resurrection.

The very same God who revealed Himself to Abraham and Moses, who performed miracles in Egypt and parted the Red Sea—the same God who provided manna in the wilderness and brought forth Yeshua—transformed my life more than thirty years ago, and He can transform yours if you let Him. If He has already done that, then trust Him to do the same for those with whom you share your faith and pray for diligently. It may take years. It may take decades, but the Word of God will not return void.

14

GOD WANTS TO USE YOU

Embracing Yeshua is the most *Jewish* thing I have ever done. In fact, it is the most *important* thing I have ever done. The same God who changed my life more than thirty years ago still has the power to change lives today. His love is transforming the lives of Jew and Gentile alike, all over the world. And He wants to use you to show them that love and to draw them to Himself. God created you with a divine destiny to fulfill, and the only way to come into that destiny is to say yes to God and surrender yourself completely to Him.

In the first thirteen chapters of this book, I have presented the evidence that Yeshua is exactly who He claimed to be: the Messiah of Israel, the Savior of the world, and the only path to the God of Abraham, Isaac and Jacob. I hope that this evidence is helpful to you as you contemplate your own spiritual destiny and share Yeshua with your Jewish friends, family and co-workers. Many people, and this is especially true of Jewish people, will not make an emotional decision based on blind faith and often need such rational, logical arguments in order to hear the truth of God's Word.

But while I believe that the evidence is overwhelming, I cannot stress enough that these are *spiritual* truths which must be *spiritually* discerned. The only way to step into this reality is to take a step of faith—not blind faith, but educated faith. You must keep in mind that it is a spiritual battle, a spiritual decision. But truth will prevail. As Yeshua Himself said, "Then you will know the truth, and the truth will set you free" (John 8:32).

FORCING MY BELIEFS?

People who do not know me often accuse me of trying to force my beliefs on others. Over the years, numerous Jewish leaders have angrily rebuked me, saying that I have no right to tell anyone what he should or should not believe. After all, they say, Judaism is not a proselytizing religion, and we Jews do not believe in Jesus. Should you have an opportunity to share Yeshua (Jesus) with Jewish friends, you may get similar arguments.

It is true that over the centuries, religious institutions of what became known as Christianity and rabbinic Judaism have parted ways and are now completely distinct. But the reality of the Gospel message has not changed since thousands of Jews first accepted it more than two thousand years ago.

Still today, tens of thousands of Jews *do* believe in Jesus, and our numbers are growing every day. I have no desire to force my beliefs on anyone. I cannot! It is impossible. But I am compelled to share with my fellow Jews and all people that God is real and alive. That His Word is true from Genesis through Revelation, that He does change lives and can change anyone's life, Jew and non-Jew alike, no matter what their situation or attitude may be like now.

TRUTH IS TRUTH

As I said at the beginning of this book, it is impossible to prove beyond a shadow of a doubt that God exists or that Jesus is the Messiah. You will not be able to do that. No one has.

Nevertheless, truth is truth. After reviewing the body of evidence, I believe it takes more faith *not* to believe than it does to believe in a personal God who is revealed in the pages of the Holy Scriptures. As I studied the pages of the New Testament for the first time, I was shocked and amazed to discover how Jewish this book of "the Christians" really was. From the beginning genealogy of Matthew, I saw that Jesus was not the God of Christianity but was, in fact, the Son of Abraham, the Son of David and a Child of Israel.

Words are not adequate to express my amazement as I read Yeshua's own words in Matthew 15:24: "I was sent only to the lost sheep of Israel." And Matthew 10:5–6, where He told His own Jewish disciples that their mission was to their own people. Then, when I went back to the Torah, Prophets and Writings (the Tanakh), I was even more amazed to discover prophecy after prophecy that clearly revealed Yeshua as the Messiah of Israel. Indeed, I found that the first disciples all were observant Jews who had discovered the Messiah, promised in the writings of their own prophets. The historical evidence and extra-biblical writings supported the reality of the Scriptures of Yeshua Himself.

Through this process of studying the Word of God and ultimately changing my entire academic and vocational direction, I became more established in my own Jewish identity. Slowly my Jewish identity changed until it no longer was based on how the mainstream Jewish community viewed me, but rather on the reality of how God viewed me and what the Scriptures taught.

As a Messianic Jew, I see myself as a continuation of a long line of Jews who have embraced Yeshua throughout the centuries—the remnant saved by grace that Paul refers to in Romans 11:5. This remnant has endured to this day and is now flourishing.

It is my fervent prayer that, having read this book, you will come into the same reality that I have found (especially if you have not yet made that step of faith). For my believing friends, I hope that you are now better equipped to walk your Jewish friends, family members and acquaintances through a similar process, reviewing the Scriptures and learning historical facts that they may not have known before. No, you cannot prove that Yeshua is the Jewish Messiah. But you can point your friends to the truth.

DECISIONS NOW AFFECT ETERNAL DESTINY

I was motivated to write this book by my firm conviction that what a person decides to believe in this lifetime does, in fact, affect his or her eternal destiny. Yet many ignore the issue of eternal life. Some even choose to believe in heaven but not hell. Consider, if you will, these arguments:

- What if the Jewish prophet Daniel was correct when he wrote, "Multitudes who sleep in the dust of the earth will awake: some to everlasting life, others to shame and everlasting contempt" (Daniel 12:2)?

- What if Yeshua was right when He warned in Mark's gospel that there is a place of complete and total darkness where "their worm does not die, and the fire is not quenched" (Mark 9:48)?

- One cannot selectively choose to believe in parts of the Bible and discard others. To believe only in the reality of heaven, while choosing to deny the reality of hell—a place of total separation from God for eternity—does not line up with Scripture, which is full of references to hell, and is a great gamble at best! And to decide to make no decision is actually in itself a decision against.

Anyone who chooses to ignore the issue of eternity is taking a serious risk. In 1 Corinthians 15, the apostle Paul said that if what he had preached was not true, then he had wasted nothing, but if it was, then those who failed to believe would be risking everything.

Remember the story about my childhood rabbi—the one I approached with the question of what happens after we die—whose only answer was that we are climbing up a mountain and only God knows what will happen when we reach the top? Well, thanks to my relationship with Yeshua, I now can see over the mountain, and I know that there is more to life than just living, breathing, eating and dying. There is an eternity ahead! Where we spend it is determined by the decisions we make in this life now.

I pray that no one reading this book who does not yet know Yeshua will put off this decision until a more convenient hour. Such an hour may never come. And may the Lord guide you, my believing friend, to wisely and with great power and conviction, point out these truths to your Jewish friends. I want to stress again, they are not in your life by accident. God has put them there for a purpose. If you do not reach out to them and pray for them, who will? And do not put it off until tomorrow, for tomorrow may be too late.

THE HERE AND NOW

But this is not just about eternity. It is also about the here and now. I must stress again that each of us has a divine destiny! We are not here by accident! God created each one of us for a purpose. And He desires that each of us fulfills that purpose here, during our time on earth!

Yeshua promises us not only *eternal* life in the world to come, but *abundant* life now. *The Amplified Bible* defines the word *abundant* as "far over and above all that we [dare] ask or think [infinitely beyond our highest prayers, desires, thoughts, hopes, or dreams]" (Ephesians 3:20).

Abundant life is so much richer than trying to follow a bunch of laws in order to be righteous. It is about a joy and inner peace and a sense of absolute destiny that only Yeshua can provide.

FEAR OF REJECTION

One real issue we Jews have to deal with in responding to the Gospel is the fear of rejection. This fear is real and genuine. The rejection of family, friends and the entire Jewish establishment is a painful reality.

In my three decades of ministry, I have met many Jewish people who have told me they cannot accept Yeshua because they feel they would be turning their backs on their heritage or hurting their parents. Some of them have even been convinced that Yeshua is exactly who He claimed to be, the Messiah of Israel, yet they were not ready to experience the rejection that accepting Him as Messiah would bring from their family and friends.

I can relate. When I became a believer in Yeshua, I experienced no small share of rejection myself. My parents were hurt, the rabbi was angry, and many of my Jewish friends felt that I had turned my back on my heritage.

Perhaps you are having similar thoughts right now if you are Jewish. Do not let this stop you! What you will gain is so worth any rejection you may have to endure! And for my believing friends, do not be surprised if you hear similar comments from your Jewish friends. I know it will grieve you as it grieves me. There is nothing sadder than watching a Jewish person walk away for fear of rejection even when he knows in his heart that Yeshua is Israel's Messiah. Those who turn away from Yeshua are missing out on the joy, excitement and wonder that come from a personal relationship with the living God—the God of all creation.

I encourage you not to give up. Press on, and take every opportunity you have to speak truth to your Jewish friends. Keep praying for them faithfully, and leave the rest up to God.

LEADING THE WAY TO SALVATION

As you sense that someone you have been sharing with may be open to receive Yeshua into his or her life, I encourage you to share the following Scriptures with him or her. I have found these useful in my own experience:

> I am the way and the truth and the life. No one comes to the Father except through me.
> —JOHN 14:6

> Whoever believes in the Son has eternal life, but whoever rejects the Son will not see life, for God's wrath remains on him.
> —JOHN 3:36

> He who has the Son has life; he who does not have the Son of God does not have life.
> —1 JOHN 5:12

> If you confess with your mouth, "Jesus [Yeshua] is Lord," and believe in your heart that God raised him from the dead, you will be saved.
> —ROMANS 10:9

Here I am! I stand at the door and knock. If anyone hears
my voice and opens the door, I will come in and eat with him,
and he with me.

—REVELATION 3:20

When you share Yeshua with others, I encourage you to explain
that the simple process of receiving eternal life begins with the real-
ization and admission that all of us have sinned against God's law,
and therefore, all of us are guilty and separated from a holy, righteous
God. This is why Yeshua came into the world. He came to pay the
penalty for our sin once and for all and to make us righteous with
God. Here is a wonderful Scripture that says this very thing:

This righteousness from God comes through faith in
Jesus Christ [Yeshua, the Messiah] to all who believe. There is
no difference, for all have sinned and fall short of the glory of
God, and are justified freely by his grace through the redemption that came by Christ Jesus [Yeshua, our Messiah]. God
presented him as a sacrifice of atonement, through faith in his
blood.

—ROMANS 3:22–25

This passage in Romans makes it abundantly clear that forgiveness and justification for being made right before God can happen
only when a person accepts Yeshua's sacrifice through faith. How can
one do that? Again, the answer is found in the book of Romans:

If you confess with your mouth, "Jesus [Yeshua] is Lord,"
and believe in your heart that God raised him from the dead,
you will be saved. For it is with your heart that you believe and
are justified, and it is with your mouth that you confess and
are saved. As the Scripture says, "Anyone who trusts in him will
never be put to shame." For there is no difference between Jew
and Gentile—the same Lord is Lord of all and richly blesses all

who call on him, for, "Everyone who calls on the name of the
Lord will be saved."
—Romans 10:9–13

It always amazes me just how simple all of this is. It is so easy a
baby could understand it. For some, especially some Jewish people,
that is exactly what makes it so hard to believe. All a person has to
do is tell Yeshua in his own words that he wants to turn his life over
to Him and that he accepts the sacrifice Yeshua has made on his
behalf. All one has to do is to recognize his sin, ask for forgiveness
and decide to live for Yeshua. He will do the rest.

These simple steps to salvation are what the rabbis call *teshuva*,
which is most accurately defined as a turning toward God, acknowledging that you were walking in one direction (away from God),
but now in your heart you are ready to make a 180-degree turn and
spend the remainder of your life walking toward Him. This is a good
Jewish way to explain the concept of salvation. And for those who,
like me, have done this, it is a life-transforming experience that we
will never regret! I cannot encourage you strongly enough that God
wants to use you to bring others, especially your Jewish friends, into
this same life-transforming experience.

ENCOURAGING, TRUE STORIES OF MESSIANIC JEWS

Most of us who are believers in Yeshua (especially us Jewish believers)
have family, friends and loved ones who have not yet entered into
the glorious encounter with the Lord that we have. If you are like
me, you may at times become discouraged. Let me tell you about
the lives of several Jewish men whose stories are inspiring. Perhaps
you can in turn share them with your Jewish friends.

Dr. Boris Kornfeld became a believer [in his Messiah] as an
inmate in a Soviet concentration camp. While serving as the camp's

doctor, he tried to help starving prisoners by refusing to sign papers that would send them to their deaths. One day he saw a Soviet orderly stealing food from the prisoners, and he reported it to the camp commandant. Soon after he spent some time with a patient who had just been operated on for cancer, telling him all about the Messiah. That night Dr. Kornfeld was murdered by the orderly he had reported. But after his death, Dr. Kornfeld's patient continued to think about what he had said. Eventually that man surrendered his own life to Messiah. Perhaps you have heard of him. His name was **Alexandr Solzhenitsyn.**[1]

Dr. David Block was a professor of applied mathematics and astronomy in South Africa. He wrote, "I would listen in shul as the rabbis expounded how God was a personal God . . . and wondered how I fit into all of it." He wondered what had happened to the God who spoke to Abraham, Moses and the other patriarchs. "Where was the personality and the vibrancy of a God who could speak to David Block?" he says.

Dr. Block knew that God existed. As an astronomer, he became more sure of it every time he looked through a telescope and saw the order and beauty of the universe. But where was He? How did one enter into a personal relationship with Him? When he told a Christian colleague how he was feeling, the man urged him to talk to his minister. Block says:

> My parents had taught me to seek answers where they may be found, and so I consented to meet with this Christian minister. [He] read to me from the New Testament book of Romans. . . . Suddenly it all became very clear to me: Yeshua had fulfilled the Messianic prophecies in the Hebrew Scriptures. . . . I knew that Jesus was the Messiah and is the Messiah. And I surrendered my heart and my soul to Him that day.
>
> It might seem strange to some that a scientist and a Jew could come to faith in Jesus. But faith is never a leap into the

dark. It is always based on evidence. That was how my whole search for God began. I looked through my telescope at Saturn and said to myself, *Isn't there a great God out there?* The logical next step was to want to meet this Designer face-to-face.[2]

Serena Rosengarten Kiss is another well-known Jew who became a follower of Messiah.

Kiss was born into a strongly religious Jewish family in Hungary. He was drawn to Yeshua by a young housekeeper, of whom he wrote, "That girl was the first genuine Christian we had met, and she represented a Christianity of which I had known nothing before." He adds, "This Christian girl was singing hymns while she scrubbed the floor, she was praying while ironing our clothes. She spent evenings in her room studying the Bible."

Kiss was offended when the housekeeper told him that Jesus was the Messiah. But through her persistent witness and his own study of the Bible, he eventually accepted Yeshua as his Messiah and Savior.

He writes:

> In spite of the perverted Christendom of past centuries and in spite of all the tragic experiences of my people during the Nazi period, I found in Jesus my Redeemer, and I committed my life to Him. He enabled me to "see the invisible, believe the incredible, expect the impossible." He graciously clothed me with the garment of salvation (see Psalm 149:4; Isaiah 61:10). He is the Logos, God's Word, the *Memra*, the *Metatron*, the *Malach Ha'Panim* (the Angel of God's Face). He is the Lamb of God who took upon Himself the sin of the world.[3]

Then there is my good friend about whom I spoke earlier, **Rose Price**, who lost her entire family, save one sister, in the Holocaust. For years, Rose was bitter and hated Germans—and all Gentiles, for that matter. She was an angry and unhappy woman, and she became even more angry and unhappy when her daughter turned her life over to Yeshua. Rose began studying the Scriptures because she wanted to prove her daughter wrong and win her back to Judaism.

Rose recounts the story in her wonderful book, *A Rose from the Ashes.*[4] In the end, Rose was transformed by the power of God and has spent the remainder of her beautiful and fulfilled life helping people learn to forgive. She is a dynamic example of the transforming power of God, who was able to take someone who experienced such horrific tragedy and deliver her into an abundant, joy-filled life.

These are only a few examples of Jews who have found new life through faith in Messiah. There are many more:

Andrew Mark Barron, an aerospace engineer who was raised in conservative Judaism but came to faith in Yeshua upon reading the New Testament, states:

> I believed God existed because of the phenomenal order to the universe, yet I felt human beings were far too miniscule for His notice. . . . Believing God cares is not intellectual suicide; believing that He does not care is spiritual starvation.[5]

Constantin Brunner, philosopher and author, writes:

> His [Yeshua's] profound and holy words, and all that is true and heart-appealing in the New Testament, must from now on be heard in our synagogues and taught to our children. . . . That He at last may find us who has always been seeking after us.

John Cournos, Jewish novelist and writer, says succinctly:

> Jesus was not only a Jew. He was the apex and acme of Jewish teaching.[6]

Norman Cousins, bestselling author and executive editor of *Saturday Review,* states:

> There is every reason for Judaism to lose its reluctance toward Jesus. His own towering spiritual presence is a projection of Judaism, not a repudiation of it. Jesus is not to be taxed for the un-Christian ideas and acts of those who have spoken in His name. Jesus never repudiated Judaism. He was proud to be a Jew, yet He did not confine Himself to Judaism. . . . No other figure—spiritual, philosophical, political or intellectual—has had a greater impact on human history.[7]

Karl Jakob Hirsh, great-grandson of a rabbi, who was raised as an Orthodox Jew, says:

> My conversion to the Messianism of Jesus has strengthened and settled me; I have lost everything I once thought I possessed, but I have gained much: my faith, and myself.[8]

Lawrence Kudlow, former undersecretary of the Office of Management and Budget, came to faith in Messiah during a battle against cocaine addiction. He says:

> As I hit bottom, I lost jobs, lost all income, lost friends, and very nearly lost my wife. I was willing to surrender and take it on faith that I had to change my life. . . . I started searching for God. All of a sudden it clicked, that . . . Jesus died for me, too.[9]

Howard Phillips, former chairman of the U.S. Office of Economic Opportunity, shares:

> I began to spend more time studying the Scripture, both Old and New Testament, and began to come to grips with the

constantly mentioned subject of blood sacrifice as the basis
for atonement for sin where God was concerned. The ultimate
blood sacrifice for sin, obviously, is Jesus. I committed my life
to Him as Lord and Savior.[10]

Jay Sekulow, attorney and chief counsel for the American Center
for Law and Justice, who discovered Yeshua after reading about the
suffering servant in Isaiah 53, says:

I kept looking for a traditional Jewish explanation that
would satisfy, but found none. The only plausible explanation
seemed to be Jesus. My Christian friends were suggesting other
passages for me to read, such as Daniel 9. As I read, my suspicion that Jesus might really be the Messiah was confirmed. . . .
I had always thought my cultural Judaism was sufficient, but
in the course of studying about the Messiah who would die as
a sin bearer, I realized that I needed a Messiah to do that for
me.[11]

These are real people whose lives have been transformed because
they took the leap of faith and became Jewish believers or Messianic Jews. It does happen; Jews can recognize and accept Yeshua as
their Messiah. And your relationship with your Jewish friends may
be the turning point in their lives. May these stories inspire you to
continue in the good fight and to continue to reach out to them
with the love of Yeshua.

PLANTING THE SEEDS

As one who has a relationship with God, you may be the seed sower
in your Jewish friend's life. Allow me to relate an early experience
with the Gospel during my teenage years.

A group called Young Life was sponsoring a weeklong trip to
Colorado, and I was invited to join them. Although I did not believe

as they did, the trip they offered came at the right price for me—free. And so I went. For five days, I heard messages about this Jesus, how He walked on water, performed miracles and healed the sick. And while I was impressed with Jesus as a person, I was a Jew, and Jews did not believe in Jesus.

One night the speaker challenged us to go out by ourselves to pray and talk to God. As a Jew, this was a new experience for me. Until this time, prayer for me required the use of a *siddur* (Jewish prayer book) from which to recite the *shema* (or "Hear O Israel," the foundational confession of our Jewish faith from Deuteronomy 6:4 that declares the Lord is One, along with other prepared prayers). The concept of actually talking directly to God was completely foreign to me, as I had been taught that He was a holy and unapproachable entity, someone "up there!" And yet I stepped out into the warm night air and finding a peaceful, moonlit stream, I looked up toward a star-filled sky and prayed.

I will never forget the words I spoke. "God, if You are real, please show Yourself to me. And if what this man has said about Jesus is true, please reveal it to me. You know that I am a Jew, and we Jews do not believe in Jesus. But if He is our Messiah, I want to know."

Five years later, following my dramatic encounter with God as a university student, He took me back in my mind to that evening in Colorado, standing in the moonlight by a slow-moving stream. He reminded me that He had now answered my prayer. He showed me that those seeds that had been planted as a teenager were indeed true—that Yeshua (Jesus) was my promised Messiah. God is faithful.

The man I heard speak about Jesus on that trip to Colorado so long ago did not witness my decision to accept Yeshua as my Messiah. But he was vital to my coming to faith. He was bold enough to share the Gospel with a Jewish teenager, and his witness began my search for My Savior. I am forever grateful.

Your Jewish friends may not want to hear what you have to say, and as I have said, they may become angry or even stand up and walk out on you. Do it anyway. Some who may be terribly angry with you right now will thank you over and over again throughout eternity that you cared enough to tell them about their Savior's love.

I encourage you to be a seed sower. While you may not see the fruit that comes, God is faithful, and He will indeed water those seeds, if you are faithful to plant them.

GOD WANTS TO USE YOU

I promise you, based on the authority of the Word of God, that if you will be faithful, bold and courageous enough to speak up and to share Yeshua, He will reveal Himself to those with whom you share, just as He did for me. My prayers go with you, that you will be equipped and prepared for the spiritual battle to which God is calling you, and that all to whom you speak will have ears to listen, eyes to see and hearts to believe. I pray that your Jewish friends will have open minds and open hearts. I pray that everyone with whom you share Yeshua will earnestly seek and find truth and enter into the promised abundant and eternal life that Yeshua offers to everyone who will simply believe.

And finally, to my Jewish friend who is reading this book and has not yet decided: Do not wait. Everything I have shared is the truth. I understand the struggle you may be feeling inside right now. I have been there. But I am more Jewish now than I ever was. Inside, you know the truth. . . . Make that step of faith. It is so simple. Today is the day of your salvation if you will just take that step.

In chapter 8 I told you about Rabbi Isaac Lichtenstein, the Hungarian rabbi who became a believer after picking up and reading a New Testament he had tossed into a corner many years earlier. I can think of no better way of ending our time together than quoting from a letter written by Rabbi Lichtenstein just a few days before his death:

> Dear Jewish brethren; I have been young, and now am old. I have attained the age of eighty years, which the Psalms speak of as the utmost period of human life on earth. When others my age are reaping with joy the fruits of their labors, I am alone, almost forsaken, because I have lifted up my voice in warning, "Return, O Israel, return unto the Lord thy God; for thou hast stumbled in thine iniquity. Take with you words and return unto the Lord" (Hosea 14:1–2).
>
> I, an honored rabbi for nearly forty years, am now in my old age treated by my friends as one possessed by an evil spirit, and by my enemies as an outcast. I am become the butt of mockers who point the finger at me. But while I live I will stand on my watchtower, though I may stand here alone. I will listen to the words of God, and look for the time when He will return to Zion in mercy, and Israel shall fill the world with His joyous cry: "Hosannah to the Son of David! Blessed is He that cometh in the name of the Lord! Hosannah in the highest!"[12]

Notes

INTRODUCTION
1. C. S. Lewis, *Mere Christianity* (London: Collins, 1952), 54–56.

CHAPTER 2
1. Arthur W. Kac, *The Messiahship of Jesus: What Jews and Christians Say* (Chicago: Moody Press, 1980), 26.
2. Alfred Edersheim, *The Life and Times of Jesus the Messiah* (Grand Rapids, Mich.: Wm B. Eerdmans Publishing, First One-Volume Printing, 1971), xii.0.1221.
3. Kac, 55.
4. Ibid.
5. Ibid., 42.
6. Jirair Tashjian, "Jesus of Nazareth and the Christ of Faith: Embracing the Journey" (June 15, 2009), http://www.crivoice.org/jesus1.html.
7. Shaye I. D. Cohen, quoted in "From Jesus to Christ," *Frontline*, WGBH Educational Foundation, April 1998, http://www.pbs.org/wgbh/pages/frontline/shows/religion/jesus/bornliveddied.html.
8. Shalom Ben-Chorin, "The Image of Jesus in Modern Judaism," *Journal of Ecumenical Studies* 11, no. 3 (Summer 1974): 408.

CHAPTER 3
1. Peter Schafer, *Jesus in the Talmud* (Princeton, N.J.: Princeton University Press, 2007), 59.
2. Josh McDowell, *Evidence That Demands a Verdict* (San Bernardino, Ca: Campus Crusade for Christ, 1972), 62–63.
3. Moishe Rosen, *Y'shua* (Chicago: Moody Press, 1982), 70.
4. Ibid.
5. Ibid., 71.
6. Ibid., 72.
7. Peter Wise, "The Trinity in the Old Testament," Internet Biblical Resources, 1999, http://www.biblicalresources.info/pages/ot1/trinityot.html.

CHAPTER 4
1. McDowell, 175.

2. Robert Anderson, *The Coming Prince* (London: Hodder & Stroughton, 1894), 127.

3. Michael Brown, *Answering Jewish Objections to Jesus* (Grand Rapids: Baker Books, 2000), 70.

CHAPTER 5

1. Kac, 248.

2. JewishEncyclopedia.com, s.v. "Ebionites" (by Kaufmann Kohler), http://www .jewishencyclopedia.com/view.jsp?artid=22&letter=E (accessed September 15, 2010).

3. Philip Schaff, *The History of the Christian Church*, vol. 2 (New York: Charles Scribner's Sons, 1910), 431.

4. Rosen, 109.

5. Ibid., 110.

6. Ibid., 112.

CHAPTER 6

1. Jewish Virtual Library, "Rabbinic Jewish Period of Talmud Development (70–500 C.E.)," The American-Israel Cooperative Enterprise, http://www.jewishvirtual library.org/jsource/History/rabbi.html.

2. Henry R. Percival, ed., "Constantine I: On the Keeping of Easter," *Internet Medieval Sourcebook*, March 23, 1997, http://www.fordham.edu/halsall/basis/nicea1.txt.

3. B. A. Robinson, "Anti-semitism: Racially-based persecution of Jews: 1800 to 1946," *Two Millennia of Jewish Persecution*, Ontario Consultants on Religious Tolerance, May 2, 2009, http://www.religioustolerance.org/jud_pers2.htm.

4. B. A. Robinson, "Anti-Judaism: 70 to 1200 CE," *Two Millenia of Jewish Persecution*, Ontario Consultants on Religious Tolerance, February 7, 2010, http://www .religioustolerance.org/jud_pers1.htm.

5. Brown, *Answering Jewish Objections to Jesus*, 126.

6. Rob Eshman, "Was Christopher Columbus a Jew?" *The Jewish Journal*, October 12, 2009, http://www.jewishjournal.com/bloggish/item/was_christopher _columbus_a_jew_20091012/.

7. Jerry Darring, "A Catholic Timeline of Events Relating to Jews, Anti-Judaism, Antisemitism, and the Holocaust From the 3rd Century to the Beginning of the Third Millennium," Theology Library at Spring Hill College, http://www.shc.edu/ theolibrary/resources/Timeline.htm.

8. Raul Hilberg, *The Destruction of the European Jews* (New York: Holmes and Meier, 1985), 4.

9. Ibid., 5.

10. Martin Luther, "On the Jews and Their Lies, 1543," *Luther's Works*, vol. 47, tr. Martin H. Bertram (Minneapolis: Augsburg Fortress, 1971), http://www.humanitas -international.org/showcase/chronography/documents/luther-jews.htm.

CHAPTER 7

1. Brown, *Answering Jewish Objections to Jesus*, 21.

2. Ibid., 21–22.

3. Ibid., 22.

4. Ibid., 148–150.

CHAPTER 8

1. Ibid., 150.

2. Ibid.

3. Ibid., 155.

4. Stephen Pacht, "Anti-Semitism in the New Testament," *Jews for Jesus*, January 1, 1993, http://www.jewsforjesus.org/publications/newsletter/1993_01/anti.

5. David H. Stern, *Jewish New Testament Commentary* (Clarksville, Md.: Jewish New Testament Publications, Inc., 1992), 617–619.

6. William Barclay, *Letters to the Seven Churches* (Louisville: Westminster/John Knox Press, 2001), 26.

7. Paul Johnson, "The Necessity of Christianity," Leadership U, July 14, 2002, http://www.leaderu.com/truth/1truth08.html.

8. Michael Brown, *Our Hands Are Stained With Blood* (Shippensburg, Pa: Destiny Image, 1992).

CHAPTER 9

1. Jay Smith, "The Bible and the Qur'an: An Historical Comparison: The Bible's Archeological Evidence," The Muslim-Christian Debate Website, 1997, http://debate.org.uk/topics/history/bib-qur/bibarch.htm.

2. Quoted in McDowell, 73.

3. Norman L. Geisler, *Baker Encyclopedia of Christian Apologetics* (Grand Rapids, Mich.: 1999), 47.

4. McDowell, 69.

5. Ibid.

6. Ibid.

7. Schafer, 64.

8. Rosen, 112.

9. McDowell, 84–85.

10. Louis H. Feldman, *Anchor Bible Dictionary* (Garden City, N.Y.: Doubleday, 1991), 990–991.

11. McDowell, 86–87.

12. Ibid., 86.

13. Phlegon, *202nd Olympiad*, quoted in Jerome's Latin translation of Eusebius' *Chronicle*, tr. Roger Pearse, http://www.tertullian.org/fathers/jerome_chronicle_03_part2.htm.

14. Quoted in McDowell, 84.

15. Suetonius, *Suetonius*, vol. 2, trans. J. C. Rolfe (New York: MacMillan Co., 1914), 111.

16. Ibid., 53.

17. Lucian, *Lucian*, vol. 5, "The Passing of Peregrinus," trans. A. M. Harmon, Loeb Classical Library (Cambridge, Mass.: Harvard University Press, 1936), 13–15.

18. Pliny, *Letters* 10.96–97, "Pliny to the Emporer Trajan," trans. James J. O'Donnell, http://www9.georgetown.edu/faculty/jod/texts/pliny.html.

19. Albert Einstein, interview by George Sylvester Viereck, "What Life Means to Einstein," *The Saturday Evening Post*, October 26, 1929, 17, quoted in Kac, 40.

20. Information on the lives of the apostles taken from William Steuart McBirnie, *The Search for the Twelve Apostles* (Wheaton, Il.: Tyndale, rev. 2008).

CHAPTER 10

1. Kac, 265.
2. Ibid., 266.
3. Brown, *Answering Jewish Objections to Jesus,* 77.
4. Ibid., 78.
5. See *Zionism and Israel—Encyclopedic Dictionary,* s.v. "Bar Kochba," http://www
   .zionism-israel.com/dic/Bar_Kochba.htm (accessed September 8, 2010).
6. JewishEncyclopedia.com, s.v. "Shabbethai Zebi B. Mordecai" (by Kaufmann Kohler, Henry Malter), http://www.jewishencyclopedia.com/view
   .jsp?artid=531&letter=S.
7. Ibid.
8. Ibid.

CHAPTER 11

1. "Karaite Fact Sheet," The Karaite Korner, May 22, 2008, http://www.karaite-korner
   .org/fact_sheet.shtml.
2. Kac, 85.
3. Ibid.
4. Ibid., 138.
5. Jona Lendering, "Wars between the Jews and Romans: Simon ben Kosiba (130–136
   CE)," Livius, http://www.livius.org/ja-jn/jewish_wars/jwar07.html.
6. Edersheim, 106.
7. Ibid., 107.
8. David R. Blumenthal, "Repentance and Forgiveness," *CrossCurrents,* http://www.cross
   currents.org/blumenthal.htm.
9. Jonathan Sacks, "Teshuva, Tefilla and Tzedakah," Chabad.org, http://www
   .chabad.org/holidays/JewishNewYear/template_cdo/aid/4453/jewish/Teshuvah
   -Tefilla-and-Tzedakah.htm.
10. Kac, 238.

CHAPTER 12

1. McDowell, 189.
2. Ibid., 367.
3. Ibid.
4. C. S. Lewis, *Surprised by Joy* (New York: Harcourt Brace Jovanovich, 1942),
   223–224.
5. C. S. Lewis, *The Collected Letters of C. S. Lewis: Family Letters, 1905–1931,* ed. Walter
   Hooper (San Francisco: HarperCollins, 2004), 977.
6. McDowell, 366.
7. Frank Morison, *Who Moved the Stone?* (Grand Rapids: Zondervan, 1987).
8. Lee Strobel, "About Lee," www.leestrobel.com.
9. Lee Strobel, *The Case for Easter* (Grand Rapids: Zondervan, 1998), 77.
10. Ibid., 8.
11. Quoted in McDowell, 217.
12. Wilbur M. Smith, *Therefore Stand* (Grand Rapids: Baker Book House, 1974), 386.
13. Raymond E. Brown, *The Virginal Conception & Bodily Resurrection of Jesus* (New
    York: Paulist Press, 1973), 126.
14. Ibid., 122.

15. Strobel, *The Case for Easter*, 76.
16. Ibid., 73–74.
17. Ibid., 21.
18. Ibid.
19. Ibid., 24–25.
20. Brad Harrub and Bert Thompson, "An Examination of the Medical Evidence for the Physical Death of Christ," ApologeticsPress.org, January 2002, http://www.apologeticspress.org/articles/119.
21. William D. Edwards, Wesley J. Gabel, and Floyd E. Hosmer, "On the Physical Death of Jesus Christ," *Journal of the American Medical Association* 255, no. 11 (1986):1455–1463.
22. James D. Tabor, "Josephus' References to Crucifixion," The Jewish Roman World of Jesus, 1998, http://religiousstudies.uncc.edu/people/jtabor/cruc-josephus.html.
23. McDowell, 208.
24. Ibid., 247.
25. Quoted in McDowell, 249.
26. Gary R. Habermas, "Explaining Away Jesus' Resurrection: The Recent Revival of Hallucination Theories," *Christian Research Journal* 23, no. 4 (2001).
27. Strobel, *The Case for Easter*, 77.

CHAPTER 13

1. Quoted in R. Albert Mohler Jr., "Must We Believe the Virgin Birth?" The Christian Post, December 19, 2006, http://www.christianpost.com/article/20061219/must-we-believe-the-virgin-birth/index.html.
2. Schafer, 18.
3. Ibid.
4. Lee Strobel, *The Case for Faith* (Grand Rapids: Zondervan, 2000), 82–83.
5. Ibid.
6. Ibid., 117.

CHAPTER 14

1. The Association of Messianic Congregations, "A Historical Survey of Prominent Jewish Believers in Messiah Yeshua," www.messianicassociation.org/profiles.
2. David Block, "For Heaven's Sake: A Jewish Astronomer's Odyssey," *ISSUES: A Messianic Jewish Perspective* 7, no. 8 (1991).
3. Kac, 325–327.
4. Rose Price, *A Rose from the Ashes* (San Francisco: Purple Pomegranate Productions, 2006).
5. The Association of Messianic Congregations, "A Historical Survey of Prominent Jewish Believers in Messiah Yeshua," www.messianicassociation.org/profiles.
6. Kac, 32.
7. Ibid., 39.
8. Ibid., 324.
9. The Association of Messianic Congregations, "A Historical Survey of Prominent Jewish Believers in Messiah Yeshua," www.messianicassociation.org/profiles.
10. Ibid.
11. Ibid.
12. Ibid.

JONATHAN BERNIS is president and CEO of Jewish Voice Ministries International, located in Phoenix, Arizona. A native of Rochester, New York, Jonathan grew up in a traditional Jewish family and had a Bar Mitzvah at the age of thirteen. He is a graduate of the University of Buffalo and went on to obtain degrees in theology, Jewish studies and early Christianity. He also has completed extensive post-graduate work in archeology, including excavations in Israel. Jonathan hosts a weekly television program, *Jewish Voice with Jonathan Bernis*, which is broadcast throughout the United States, Canada, Israel and other countries in Europe and Asia. He speaks at dozens of conferences every year, serves on the boards of several organizations that minister in Israel and holds dual U.S./ Israeli citizenship. He has led more than thirty teaching tours to Israel and is author of *A Rabbi Looks at the Last Days*, which has recently gone into its third printing. Jonathan lives in Phoenix with his wife and children.